Interrupting Racis

MW01030186

Interrupting Racism provides school counselors with a brief overview of racial equity in schools and practical ideas that a school-level practitioner can put into action. The book walks readers through the current state of achievement gap and racial equity in schools and looks at issues around intention, action, white privilege, and implicit bias. Later chapters include interrupting racism case studies and stories from school counselors about incorporating stakeholders into the work of racial equity. Activities, lessons, and action plans promote self-reflection, staff-reflection, and student-reflection, and encourage school counselors to drive systemic change for students through advocacy, collaboration, and leadership.

Rebecca Atkins, MEd, NBCT is Senior Administrator of Elementary Counseling in the Wake County Public School System, North Carolina, and served as a school counselor for 12 years. She is a frequent presenter at state and national conferences and has published on the topics of transition and equity.

Alicia Oglesby, MS is a professional high school counselor in Washington, DC. With an extensive background in serving low-income black communities, she continues to advocate for equity on the local and national level.

Interrupting Racism

Equity and Social Justice in School
Counseling

Rebecca Atkins and Alicia Oglesby

Routledge
Taylor & Francis Group

NEW YORK AND LONDON

First published 2019
by Routledge
52 Vanderbilt Avenue, New York, NY 10017

and by Routledge
2 Park Square, Milton Park, Abingdon, Oxon, OX14 4RN

Routledge is an imprint of the Taylor & Francis Group, an informa business

© 2019 Taylor & Francis

Library of Congress Cataloging-in-Publication Data
Names: Atkins, Rebecca, author. | Oglesby, Alicia, author.
Title: Interrupting racism : equity and social justice in school
counseling / Rebecca Atkins and Alicia Oglesby.
Description: New York, NY : Routledge, 2019. | Includes
bibliographical references and index.
Identifiers: LCCN 2018034993 (print) | LCCN 2018036832
(ebook) | ISBN 9781351258920 (E-book) | ISBN 9780815366393
(hardback) | ISBN 9780815366416 (pbk.)
Subjects: LCSH: Educational counseling–Social aspects–United
States. | Educational equalization. | Social justice–Study and
teaching.
Classification: LCC LB1027.5 (ebook) | LCC LB1027.5 .A845 2019
(print) | DDC 371.4–dc23
LC record available at https://lccn.loc.gov/2018034993

ISBN: 978-0-815-36639-3 (hbk)
ISBN: 978-0-815-36641-6 (pbk)
ISBN: 978-1-351-25892-0 (ebk)

Typeset in Bembo
by Wearset Ltd, Boldon, Tyne and Wear

To our families, who gave us the gift of time to write about our passion for equity.

Contents

Foreword

For over a hundred years, school counseling or guidance counseling has been a profession known for its mission to help all students achieve academically, socially, and vocationally. Nevertheless, school counselors are rarely discussed in terms of their ability to help students who are negatively affected by biased and racist systems and policies in schools. How can one be charged with "helping" and not address the inherent policies that further divide students and communities? Although counselor educators and school counseling leaders have begun to talk about issues pertaining to social inequities through the lens of social justice and advocacy, disrupting inequities and inequalities in schools has not been perceived as a major role or responsibility of school counselors.

Over the last decade, racism in the U.S. has been evidenced by the rise in hate crimes, the blatant shootings of unarmed Black men by the police, and open and direct xenophobic rhetoric by politicians and government officials. There's no denying that bias, prejudice, and racism are prevalent in our society and in our schools. The question for school counselors has become, "how can school counselors, like other school-based educators, ensure a non-biased, anti-racist, and inclusive school environment for all students?"

This book provides school counselors with answers to the aforementioned question. The authors take care to describe the context and historical significance of academic trends in the U.S. so that the reader better understands existing achievement and opportunity gaps. Next, the authors introduce the reader to factors that influence disparities in education—white privilege and implicit bias—along with scenarios for the reader to imagine and visualize the factors playing out in schools.

My career has been focused on "leveling the playing field" for our most vulnerable students by challenging education policies that further divide people into the "haves and have nots." Creating new norms, practices, and mindsets is the key to dismantling racist and biased practices in schools. This book is a good step in that direction.

Cheryl Holcomb-McCoy, PhD
Dean, School of Education, American University

Preface

One of my favorite stories to tell is how Alicia and I began our work together on equity and social justice. You see, we met on Twitter. We were both participating in a Twitter chat for school counselors about equity. Alicia was interested in presenting at the American School Counselor Association (ASCA) national conference and was seeking advice. I had presented at ASCA a few times and was familiar with the application process. Once we started direct messaging, we decided that we would co-present. Alicia lives in Washington, DC and I live in North Carolina. We spoke on the phone, wrote an article for the ASCA School Counselor magazine, and sent many texts and emails, but we never met until we arrived in New Orleans in 2016 for the ASCA Conference.

Luckily, we hit it off and found that not only do we appreciate each other professionally but we enjoy one another's company. Alicia continues to inspire me every day that we work together. She is so knowledgeable and continues her learning each and every day. I think our unique perspectives complement each other. I work in Elementary, she works in Secondary. She has deep knowledge about the history and practice of social justice, I have deep knowledge of the ASCA National Model and systems change. I am white, she is black. I have learned more in writing this book than I ever could have going it alone.

The work of interrupting racism and fighting for equity is never done. There is always room to grow. No one can master all parts of cultural competency and mistakes are inevitable. I am humbly seeking to better understand myself and others, and to develop the complex skills to work toward equity. I am a constant work in progress. Only regular practice of questioning, learning, and engaging across difference can decrease my bias and prejudice that still show up in my daily thoughts, words, and actions. I accept this reality and keep practicing.

It's rather daunting as a white woman to write a book about equity. I struggled with the idea that I should even attempt to speak about something that I have had the privilege to struggle little with. I am white and carry my white privilege with me around the world. I am a woman but work in a field dominated by women. It was when I read the article "I've Never Experienced White Guilt" by Sarah Webb, that I realized that no one group has the answers or the whole story. In this piece, she talks about the care and preparation needed for her to be able to teach about racism and racial privilege. Something clicked for me when I read, "those oppressed within a society do not automatically have the perspective, tools and skills to critique the oppressive nature of that society" (Webb, 2018). It seemed to me that no one automatically has the tools they need to critique oppression and society. I was not required to have the answers but I was required, as a white ally, to actively work for change.

I recently attended a book study where one of the participants shared that stepping out of our comfort zones allows us to expand our circle of resources for all types of challenges we might face. The same week, I heard Chris Emdin, author of *White Folks Who Teach in the Hood*, speak and he said: "we integrated our schools without integrating our pedagogy." How powerful are those two concepts together? We put everyone in the same circle without expanding it, and some kids were left out. This is the work of my career and I will continue to try to expand my practices to benefit all students.

Rebecca Atkins

A professor in my school counseling certification program suggested our class subscribe to Twitter and use the social media platform as a professional tool. Already familiar with the site, I quickly changed my profile to reflect the new, career-focused, school counselor that I had just become. To my surprise, many counselors were already using Twitter to connect with other educators, discuss innovative ideas, and plan trips to conferences. Along came Rebecca. I had no idea at that time, exchanging similar thoughts and goals, that we'd come to where we are today. A metaphor for the typical life of a school counselor, the beginning of our journey was unpredictable, revealing, and truly exciting.

As a black woman from the urban area of Philadelphia, I grew up surrounded by an on-and-off-again relationship with diversity. My family is predominantly black. My neighborhood is predominantly black. The schools which I attended were very racially and economically diverse. Starting out in Catholic school, I was raised and educated as, numerically at least, a minority. I can remember white classmates trying to braid my hair with little to no success. My single mother did her best to help my six-year-old self understand the differences between people while insuring my self-esteem was intact. Growing up, I had a number of black female role models to aspire to. Many nights spent watching "Family Matters," "A Different World," and "Living Single" led me to connect to wholesome, assertive, and professional people who are supportive, involved, and highly educated. Attending one of the most diverse public magnet high schools in Philadelphia only strengthened my racial identity. I shared classroom space and talking time with students who identified as Nigerian, Cambodian, Laotian, Puerto Rican, Haitian, Brazilian, Kenyan, and French, to name a few. We didn't just surround ourselves with difference and highlight it in statistics, we celebrated difference. Everyone was represented in some way. When I entered Howard University, I appreciated difference and was given room to be myself in ways I had not yet experienced. My professors were black and the most thoughtfully educated people I had ever met. Sitting in lecture halls with statisticians from Port-au-Prince, reading in the library with track and field stars from Eritrea, and eating in Blackburn with "Georgia peaches" who were the third in their family to earn doctorates, filled me with confidence.

Because of my history in education, my view of race was deeply informed at an early age. The work of interrupting racism in education has evolved into a life goal. All points of my life have led to this book. The birth of my children as I walk with them through their predominantly white schools is a testament that this work remains timely and necessary. As a high-school counselor in Washington, DC, I have encountered educators craving the information that Rebecca, myself, and many other authors are attempting to provide. Rebecca and I successfully tested our first writing with the American School Counselor Association's magazine article "Mythbusters: Five Facts about Race and Racism in Schools" (ASCA, 2016). My hope is that we affirm many who are already building their profession and personal lives around social justice and equity. I also hope that, through this book, we awaken many educators who need an enthusiastic, firm, yet gentle push to be steadfast in beginning this journey.

Alicia Oglesby

Reference

Webb, Sarah (Spring, 2018). I've never experienced white guilt. *Teaching Tolerance*, 58, 54–58.

Introduction

Equity and equality are often used synonymously, but they are far from the same thing. Equality is everyone receiving the same thing. The Miriam Webster Dictionary defines equity as "freedom from bias or favoritism." In this book, we will explore the system of schooling, its inequities, and search for equity. We will look at the insidious reality of white privilege and its effect on bias. We will reflect on how school counselors can be agents of change in their school and interrupt racism when they see it.

So how do we define racism? Racism is not simply the dislike or hate of another person. Racism is about systems that marginalize people of color. It's a systemic issue. Because of this, racism is a force only acted upon people of color and "reverse racism" cannot exist. In our chapter on white privilege, we will explore how the systems of our society were created to privilege white people and the culture of white people. We will discuss how this privilege and racism is not the same as prejudice.

In *Developing Social Justice Literacy: An Open Letter to Our Colleagues*, Sensoy and Diangelo discuss shared principles of social justice education (Sensoy & Diangelo, 2009, p. 350):

- There are very real differentials in access to social and institutional power between relationally positioned group members.
- While all people have socialized prejudices and can discriminate, only the dominant group is backed by social and institutional power, which is multi-dimensional and constantly operating, being contested, and renegotiated.
- Those who claim to be for social justice must also be engaged in self-reflection on their own socialization into patterns of oppression and continually seek to counter those patterns. This is a lifelong project and is not achieved at the completion of an article or workshop.

We affirm these shared principles and seek to incorporate them into this work. The reading of this book will be challenging and, at times, difficult. We embrace this and honor the process. We firmly believe that if you are not actively seeking to interrupt racism, you are contributing to its perpetuation. We can not have a race-neutral solution to a race problem. We must step out of the taboo of race and begin the work.

Reference

Sensoy, Ö., & Diangelo, R. (2009). Developing social justice literacy: An open letter to our faculty colleagues. *Phi Delta Kappan, 90*(5), 345–352.

Part I

Building a Foundation of Understanding

Chapter 1

A Brief History

Integration, The Achievement Gap, and Student Success

What we think we may know about educating black children, educating all children to dismantle racism, may indeed be incorrect, unhelpful, and sometimes even hurtful. There are educators who fully embrace the role of providing equity to marginalized groups. There are also educators who need to identify why this role is crucial to our work. This book is for educators and school counselors who are open to the possibility that they may have not figured it all out just yet. This book is for teachers, counselors, and administrators who plan to cultivate the kind of school where children graduate nourished, fulfilled, critically thinking, and well-educated, in spite of a society that often diminishes their worth.

The history of the achievement gap begins with integration. The pivotal Brown v. Board of Education ruling was a milestone in our nation's history, with many court cases happening simultaneously from coast to coast. Black students were entering white schools. Local governments responded while the federal government had the last word. Ultimately, schools were forced to integrate despite plenty of disapproval. In the midst of the fury were students, teachers, and administrators, as school counseling was still a developing profession.

The remnants of our American educational past influence policy, classroom management, school counseling curriculum, educator-student relationships, engagement, and so much more. They influence our practice. Daily news stories remind us of the racial tensions that still permeate our school buildings and stifle our progress. Our primary resolve is to break free from the influence of the evils of the past (and present). Through continued work and exploration, new habits can form. When we understand and recognize the biases that influence our thinking and behavior, we can help our communities, regardless of their race, work against the biases that hinder our progress as a nation. We must take the lead from schools and educators who are already succeeding in this work. They have so much to teach us if we are only willing to listen, act, and innovate. Only then can we do the necessary action of dismantling systems that do not benefit all races, creeds, and cultures.

Contemporary Corrections

Let's be fair. Schools and educators are getting a lot right. With all that is happening in the United States, it is easy to ignore the major strides we have taken as a society towards social justice and equity. It is our intention to start with positive examples before moving into the history of segregation and educational shortcomings, because we firmly believe in the ability of the educational system to overcome its negative past. Let's review some contemporary examples. Over 300 teachers and principals attended a conference during the summer of 2017 focusing on integration, whiteness, and inclusion within schools. Hosted by Teachers College, Columbia University in New York City, hundreds of educators gathered and collaborated for a common interest: reducing the impact of racism on the lives of students. Educators from across the country spent days learning, discussing, and calling into action ways to dismantle racism in their schools. The title of the workshop "Reimagining Education: Teaching and Learning in Racially Diverse Schools" gave educators an opportunity to learn about race and education. The topic "Deconstructing Racial Microaggressions within Educational Settings" identified and sought to teach educators how to prevent the damaging effects of microaggressions against people of color (Buque, 2017). Additional topics such as "Redefining Culturally Relevant Mentoring as Part of Educational Leadership Development" addressed the need for education professionals to increase their race literacy (Smith, 2017). The workshops facilitators offered resources, information, guidance, and outcomes.

During the winter months of 2017, a school district near Rochester, New York offered a free viewing of the film "I'm Not Racist … Am I?" (Lee & Greene, 2014). By showing the film, the district made a clear communication to the community: they want students and families to think about and discuss race. They want their students and families to know that race will be confronted in one way or another: positively through intentional practices or negatively by happenstance. Community members of the New York school districts of Fairport, West Irondequoit, Penfield, and Pittsford were able to view the film as a group and process the effects of racism on their lives. The leaders within this district likely encountered the kind of resistance we will address in Chapter 10. Thankfully, the pushback did not take precedence over the need for showing the film. District leaders in this instance were courageous about confronting racism.

Other examples include "The Race Institute of K-12 Educators," who maintain an advisory board that consists of educators from Russell Byers Charter School, Episcopal Academy, and Palumbo High School, all within the Philadelphia, Pennsylvania region. The advisory board is consistently involved with issues related to diversity and inclusion throughout public, charter, and private institutions. An education writer featured on the site and used as a topic of discussion is Melinda Anderson, who wrote an article titled "When Educators Understand Race and Racism" (2014). She quotes an educational leader who said:

> The notion of care is the root of racial proficiency. I want to know who you are. You're not fully caring for kids if you don't know them. So race is something that we talk about. Culture is something that we talk about. Understanding that difference is an amazing, powerful plus that, if we nurture it, makes us all smarter than we can be separately.
>
> (Anderson, 2014, final para.)

The Bank Street School for Children (BSSC) on the Upper West Side of Manhattan in New York City provides a concrete and thorough approach for schools to cover these themes of race. At BSSC, students are directly involved in learning about privilege, affinity, and inclusion throughout the school day. Despite an area as racially diverse as New York City, the Bank School's parents and surrounding community initially disapproved of the racially conscious program. The lack of support did not deter school officials who knew the value and importance of teaching children how to navigate issues of race and difference. In Newton Public Schools, located in an affluent area of Massachusetts, school leadership incorporated anti-bias curriculum to further develop ideas of racial inclusion and critical thinking over a decade ago. Adapting multicultural approaches to subjects such as mathematics and science proved to be a way children can view themselves as a part of learning. The Newton website is clear about their value, stating: "GOAL 2: EDUCATIONAL EQUITY: Narrow achievement gaps with respect to race, ethnicity and socioeconomic status and increase the achievement of students with special needs" (Newton Public Schools, 2016).

An ambitious elementary school counselor led equity efforts within her small predominantly white elementary school in Ames, Iowa. As the school counselor, Riley Drake of Ames, Iowa created a program where students audit the books in their library based on skin tones and ethnicity. Students tally the representation of race and culture in books to find what is missing. They then order new books to fill in the gaps.

> What prompted my inquiry about our library was the nonfiction section, which included limited texts about a few people who were involved in historical movements for civil rights. We had the usuals: Rosa Parks, MLK Jr., and Jackie Robinson, but there were so many incredible people missing who are often overlooked because of the heroistic mentality used that discourages our students from believing that they can in fact enact change. I was concerned about how this narrowed the conceptualization of the movement for our students and began investigating our other sections. This was when I discovered that while our library was packed with ... recommendations from book orders and their website[s], we were missing representation of so many of our students. For example, unless the book was about slavery, it was unlikely that a Black student would read about a character who looked like them. The books about slavery were often whitewashed, too. Instead of going through the library and demanding an examination of each text, I used an equity literacy approach and proposed the idea to students, who readily agreed. They analyzed the texts and determined what was missing. They then spoke to what THEY believed our library needed. It was an opportunity to teach critical analysis and how to collectively organize to affect change.
>
> (R. Drake, personal communication, June 6, 2018)

Lastly, Professional School Counselors of Color (PSCOC) is a designated space for school counselors who identify as non-white. Members can gather to discuss issues related to being a person of color in a predominantly white profession. Through social media conversations, emotional support, and networking, the group offers its members a chance to collectively engage. Mekisha Hughes, a school counselor and the founder of PSCOC, sought to provide a welcoming environment where common experiences could be shared. Today, the administration team includes Mekisha, Carletta S. Hurt, Kimberly Brown, and Alicia Oglesby. Collaboratively, the group manages social media outlets, a website, conference events, and school counselor trainings with American University.

Teachers, counselors, principals, and collaborators all over the country have been involved in improving the wellbeing of students since the early stages of school integration. Educators of all races and backgrounds have always found ways in which they can further the notion that all children deserve quality education regardless of race. Educators are on the front line of helping students and families understand the detriment of racism while working to dismantle it. These traditions are upheld throughout the nation in complex, creative, and innovative ways. We hope to expand that work and continue to promote healthier schools through our race-specific suggestions and interventions. Let us now explore ways in which we can improve based on what has *not* worked very well within education and school counseling.

A Brief History of Race: Education and School Counseling

Education

We have to take a brief but mighty step back into history to reveal how we arrived at the present state of education and school counseling. Since the founding of this nation, education has been separate and unequal. During the enslavement of black and indigenous people, only whites were legally allowed to read and write. In the late 1950s, movements across the nation were devoted to civil rights, including education. Nine black students in Little Rock, Arkansas were chosen to integrate an all white secondary school. Ernest Green, Elizabeth Eckford, Jefferson Thomas, Terrence Roberts, Carlotta Walls LaNier, Minnijean Brown, Gloria Ray Karlmark, Thelma Mothershed, and Melba Pattillo Beals were met with anger and hatred by white parents who did not want their students attending school with black children. The Arkansas governor at that time, Orval Faubus, called the Arkansas National Guard to block the entrance of the black students. President Eisenhower, as a courageous response to that call, sent the 101st Airborne Infantry to open the doors of Central High School to the black students. In response to forced integration, Little Rock closed all the city's high schools for the 1958–59 school year, known as "The Lost Year." The district chose to deny schooling to 3,665 students rather than to integrate their schools. Teachers worked in empty classrooms. Private schools opened for white students but no private schools were opened for black students. Integration was viewed as negative and dangerous.

On November 14, 1960, six-year-old Ruby Bridges walked into her first day of at William Frantz Elementary surrounded by angry, hate-filled adults who were determined to undo the Brown v. Board of Education decision to integrate. Up until this day, despite the federal law, schools remained all-white. Imagine: a small brown-skinned child on her way to her first day of school hearing mobs shout that she is not wanted and she does not belong, even after passing an exam to allow her admission into the school. The sign of these times was clear: black students and white students were not to learn and grow and thrive together even after the law says they should.

Little is known or taught about the three students known as The McDonogh Three (Cave, 2017). Also in New Orleans, around the same time as Ruby Bridges, Leona Tate, Tessie Prevost, and Gail Etienne entered McDonogh No. 19, an all-white elementary school. Based on zoning, the three girls were supposed to be attending McDonogh No. 19 anyway, but racial segregation was being upheld. Once again, federal authorities stepped in to escort the girls to school. Similar to the response at Frantz Elementary, white parents removed their children from school while teachers continued to teach and the faculty continued to work. Today, those nine teenagers in Little Rock, the late Ruby Bridges, the McDonough Three among many others are lauded as heroes for their actions. Thankfully, over time, opinions and beliefs changed.

Since the 1954 Brown v. Board ruling, we have learned that legal decisions fail to create a new culture. Laws are meant to fix what may be broken within a society. Laws do not, however, fix what may be broken within an individual's beliefs and ideas. Schools across the country saw drastic demographic changes but no demographic changes in communities and neighborhoods. Families were not accustomed to racially diverse experiences, especially in neighborhood communities, as redlining, discussed in detail in Chapter 2, was still a very common and systematic practice at the time, keeping black people out of white neighborhoods. In a region as globally diverse as Washington, DC, private education enrollment soared as white families fled from public schools where black and brown children began to enroll. The peak of private school enrollment occurred in 1971. Many attributed the rise to the baby-boomer generation and their growing families, but private education was tuition-based. In 2016, the Southern Education Foundation found the rise in private school enrollment was directly related to the integration of schools (SEA, 2016). The laws changed but minds did not, and parents were willing to pay tuition for their child to be educated in a segregated environment (National Center for Education Statistics, 1993).

School Counseling

The history of school counseling is just as peppered with racial tension, though little research exists on the impact of integration on school counseling specifically. Stephens & Lindsey (2011, p. 15) write:

> The school counseling profession as we know it today found its origin in the early 1900s in vocational guidance. The United States was in the throws of protest and reform stemming from "negative social conditions" of the Industrial Revolution [...]. The necessity of teaching students from divergent backgrounds and preparing them for gainful employment in an industrialized nation led, very appropriately, to the emergence of vocational guidance in schools.

Schools were at this time still not legally integrated and the divergent backgrounds mentioned are likely to be amongst white student bodies. The school counseling profession was designed and shaped in predominantly white schools by white counselors to reflect the needs of the working class. Programs, such as the National Defense Education Act, were funded by the government to train counselors leading into the 1950s to address growing poverty as veterans returned from war and migration occurred away from southern states. Again, these were programs created in predominantly white institutions for white students.

In response, the American School Counselor Association (ASCA) was formed.

> In an effort to unify and formalize the school counseling profession, the American School Counselor Association was established in 1958…. ASCA redefined the profession of school counseling as separate from teaching. By the 1960s, this redefinition led to the hiring of more full time school counselors to provide guidance and counseling services in schools, this moving from the prior trend of teachers being assigned counseling duties.
>
> (Stephens & Lindsay, 2011, p. 18)

Imagine: as more black students are moving into white schools, new school counselors are being trained and hired to support every student in their school regardless of race. Equity has yet to become a crucial component of practice although equality is a likely goal. It is unknown if the schools of the Little Rock Nine, Ruby Bridges, and the McDonogh Three had school counselors and what their roles were in the integration of black students.

School Counselors As Leaders in Race Equity

The contemporary role of the school counselor is clearly defined, structured, and modeled. The Education Trust of 1996 states that school counseling is "a profession that focuses on the relations and interactions between students and their school environment to reduce the effects of environmental and institutional barriers that impede student academic success" (Education Trust, 2009, definition). Unpacking this definition we are led to two (among many other) primary themes as they relate to this book: (1) relationships with students and (2) reduction of institutional barriers. We will continue to explore those themes in Chapters 4 and 8 respectively. Prior to the Education Trust, and even ASCA, no clearly defined supports were in place to account for integration. If they were, they were not explicitly outlined in school counselor training. Romano, Goh, and Wahl (2005, p. 114) tell us that

> the civil rights and women's liberation movements … called for school counselors to place attention on student diversity and special needs…. The importance of serving youth within schools to maximize their potential is essential across geographical regions and cultures.

As each decade proved to include an influx of immigrants and as integration became federally mandated, the necessity to learn a more multicultural approach was apparent (Holcomb-McCoy, 1999). ASCA identifies the school counselor as school leadership. The role must "provide data on student outcomes, showing achievement gaps and provide leadership for schools to view data through an equity lens" (Stephens & Lindsey, 2011, p. 38).

The Resurgence of Segregation and the Continued Achievement Gap

The Resurgence of Segregation

Presently, schools throughout the country are as segregated as they were prior to Brown v. Board of Education. A recent article in the *New York Times* by Nikole Hannah-Jones explores the segregation of Jefferson County, Alabama (2017). The ways in which language is used to describe neighborhoods and neighborhood schools is a means to perpetuate racial separations. For example, Hannah-Jones discussed a southern community's attempt to keep separate from a larger school district under the guise of achievement, local control, and safety when, in reality, the majority of the white community simply did not want to integrate with a larger, more diverse system. The misuse of achievement theories, local government, and crime statistics are ways in which groups impose racism against black communities.

A common misunderstanding of achievement is that black students are less intelligent than white students, across socioeconomic status, and that this lack of intelligence is to blame for the achievement gap. Achievement gap is defined by the National Education Association (NEA) as "the differences between the test scores of minority and/or low-income students and the test scores of their White and Asian peers" (NEA, 2017). Another common misconception is that black neighborhoods are more violent than white neighborhoods without taking into account issues related to poverty and access to weapons. For example, mass school shootings in the United States have only occurred at predominantly white schools.

These common misconceptions and faulty ideas about schools and black students have proven to be fuel for the plight of re-segregation in America. The Jefferson County school district in Alabama is one example of a white community legally protesting the admission of black students into its schools. "What the Gardendale case [in Jefferson County, Alabama] demonstrates with unusual clarity is that changes in the law have not changed the hearts of many white Americans" (Hannah-Jones, 2017, final paragraph). As the historian Bagley wrote, when it comes to school segregation, "there would be no moral awakening" (cited in Hannah-Jones, 2017). Judge Madeline Hughes-Haikala, the presiding judge in the Gardendale v. Jefferson County case, stated:

> History teaches that communities, left to their own devices, resegregate fairly quickly.... In doing the complicated work of dissolving a desegregation order, a court must ensure that the dying embers of de jure segregation aren't once again fanned into flames.
>
> (Hannah-Jones, 2017)

De jure in this case means legally recognized segregation. Throughout the country, the rise of segregation continues, particularly with no intentional effort to integrate.

The Continued Achievement Gap

An opportunity to highlight and explain the academic differences between groups of students was also born from integration efforts. The effects of large-scale demographic changes in schools forced an emergence of new philosophies, new policies, and new perspectives. The National Assessment of Educational Progress (NAEP) was created in the 1960s following mandated integration to evaluate academic trends across the nation. The assessments were designed to provide a window into how well students were learning across many differences, including race. Due to discriminatory hiring practices, educators in public schools across the country were largely white. According to a study by the Harvard Educational Review, Black educators were not being hired at the rate of white teachers despite similar teacher education (D'amico, Pawlewicz, Earley, & McGeehan, 2017). An overall understanding of how and what students learn became a necessity as teachers were tasked to educate a changing demographic of students. Because neighborhoods are still largely segregated by race, cross-cultural interaction outside of school is rare. Capturing data across gender, race, and other characteristics became a way in which the larger society and educational institutions could evaluate education. The data collected uncovered disparities. The academic difference between white students and black students leads to a continuum of interpretations. To further understand the achievement gap, we need to first acknowledge the biases and beliefs we hold as individuals and as a society. Let's explore two perspectives: standardized assessment and holistic assessment.

Standardized Assessment

The first perspective of achievement is through standardized assessment. In this philosophy, students have a standard course of study and are assessed in a standard manner to determine the efficacy of instruction and level of mastery by students. The word "standardized" means "compared to a standard." As we have seen in the history of integration, the standard is that of white mainstream society, as education in its earliest forms has been created by white educators for white students. This perspective of achievement is limited because it fails to incorporate the complex reality of postsecondary success, the ideal measured outcome of education.

The Bell Curve (Herrnstein & Murray, 1994) was published when controversial science, a widening achievement gap, and a standard of integrated schools were at their height. Highlighting this text gives us an opportunity to examine systemic influences as they relate to the continued beliefs about black and brown communities. Education professionals, sociologists, and psychologists craved literature to help explain the gaps that existed between black and white students, academically, behaviorally, and economically. Intense arguments ensued as the book only further corroborated common myths and distortions about race and class without giving deserved credence to the legal, educational, and economic systems in place.

The Bell Curve argued that human potential is marked by an "ethnic difference in cognitive ability and social behavior ... to what has been become known as the underclass" (Herrnstein & Murray, 1994, p. 267), as if the human condition is not incredibly complex, influenced by historical experiences, and greatly affected by both nature and nurture. The book provided a simplistic overview that was, in many critiques, minimizing the black experience.

> College weeds out many students, disproportionately the least able … a high proportion of people with poor test scores—more than 20 percent in the second decile for example—entered a 2-year or 4-year college. But fewer than 2 percent of them actually completed a bachelor's degree…. So a variety of forces have combined to ensure that a high percentage of the nations most able youths got into the category of college graduates.
>
> (Herrnstein & Murray, 1994, p. 36)

The historical context that contributed to disparities in college completion were largely dismissed or excluded from the book. Behavioral differences were explained by stating that "high cognitive ability is generally associated with socially desirable behaviors, low cognitive ability with socially undesirable behaviors" (Herrnstein & Murray, 1994, p. 117).

What critics would argue is that this belief system relies too heavily on genetic influences and not enough on societal influences. This belief system, still held by many scientists and educators alike, excludes groups of people from accessing educational opportunities. One author of *The Bell Curve*, Charles Murray, defended his stance by stating:

> There is a mean difference in black and white scores on mental tests, historically about one standard deviation in magnitude on IQ tests (IQ tests are normed so that the mean is 100 points and the standard deviation is 15). This difference is not the result of test bias, but reflects differences in cognitive functioning. The predictive validity of IQ scores for educational and socioeconomic outcomes is about the same for blacks and whites.
>
> (Goodnow, 2014)

Murray does not believe in racial bias or testing bias which has become a largely accepted occurrence in educational testing communities for close to a decade. The authors' perspective is incredibly problematic because it fails to account for cultural difference, historical oppression, and the traumatic effects of racism on communities of color.

Author and historian Nicholas Lemann offers this final consideration regarding standardized assessments such as the IQ test: "having conditioned its audience to view IQ as all-important, *The Bell Curve* then manipulates statistics in a way that makes IQ look bigger, and everything else smaller, in determining Americans' life-chances" (Lemann, 1997). Murray's beliefs are completely against what informs our best practice as educators and school counselors; we know that IQ does not automatically predict life outcomes. They disempower us as agents of change.

Examining education and race is incredibly problematic when done without a social justice lens, specifically social, economic, institutional, and legal injustices according to race. Factors such as racism are frequently discounted and minimized to the detriment of our students. Still, current text and educational training do not do enough to factor in the effects of racism on how we socialize children, academically and otherwise. What remains is a stigma that wherever there are black and brown children, bad things happen. Because many communities of color continue to struggle with discriminatory hiring practices, generational poverty, and mass incarceration leading to imprisonment of one parent, the issues related to poverty certainly affect learning and behavior. However, the achievement gap persists despite socioeconomic status, which means that according to the standardized assessment and regardless of income, white students are producing intended outcomes at a greater rate than black students. This is further examined through a holistic assessment approach.

Holistic Assessment

Contemporary educational philosophies reflect more student-centered, socially conscious, and holistic ideas. A student enters the school coming from a context that they did not create but to which they must adapt. Contemporary researchers and educators who hold this perspective include G. Ladson-Billings, C. Holcomb-McCoy, Christopher Emdin, Howard Stevenson, and Shaun Harper. A major component of holistic achievement is culturally relevant instruction. Dr. Ladson-Billings, a teacher educator at the University of Wisconsin-Madison, offers this precursor to understanding the achievement gap as an educational debt owed to children:

> [W]e must use our imaginations to construct a set of images that illustrate the debt. The images should remind us that the cumulative effect of poor education, poor housing, poor health care, and poor government services create a bifurcated society that leaves more than its children behind.
>
> (Ladson-Billings, 2006, p. 10)

The philosophy of educational debt is one that holds the larger society and all of its complicated layers responsible for not serving all students better, regardless of race. In Holcomb-McCoy's text *School Counseling to Close the Achievement Gap*, it is suggested that an "educator's lack of cultural competence or lack of cultural sensitivity can negatively impact the achievement of students" (2007, p. 8). Access to classrooms such as gifted and talented courses, Advanced Placement curriculum, appropriate special education, honors-level, and International Baccalaureate programs can be directly influenced by school counselors who may or may not have the cultural fluency to identify achieving students from a background different than their own.

Culturally relevant instruction at all grade levels honors the strengths that a student brings into the classroom from prior knowledge, cultural background, and skills previously acquired. Geneva Gay (2013, p. 49) focuses on culturally responsive education as "education of racially, ethnically, and culturally diverse students should connect in-school learning to out-of-school living; promote educational equity and excellence; create community among individuals from different cultural, social, and ethnic backgrounds; and develop students' agency, efficacy, and empowerment." In culturally responsive teaching, the teacher welcomes the entire learner into the process of learning and creates a relationship with the learner and their family in order to create a culture-safe environment where all students see themselves in the school. Once students are invited into the learning space, teachers view them as capable and competent. If a student struggles with learning or behavior, the teacher views this as an indicator that the instruction, curriculum, or environment needs adjustment rather than as a deficit of the student.

The task before educators and school counselors is not to determine a student's fate based on their context but to encourage the healthiest possible growth. Our position is always one of love, support, and encouragement. Teaching across difference has become more popular as educators realize that the cultural rifts in their schools and classrooms influence the learning that takes place. These rifts should not be interpreted as reason for segregation but rather an opportunity to learn, grow, and thrive inclusively.

Instead of attributing adverse childhood and life experiences to the flaws and faults of specific communities, then basing professional decisions on those attributions, we instead see each child, particularly those who have suffered, as possessing enormous potential simply because they are human. This point of view is held most notably by Ladson-Billings (2006). She urges us to dismiss the expectation that black and poor children need to play "catch up." Instead, we must examine how we have contributed to this disparity. She urges us to insure all children are learning in ways that are equitable and just (Ladson-Billings, 2006).

As educators, we often place undue responsibility on children and families to hold the weight of education despite negative historical contexts and continued economic burdens. We commonly hear educators blame poor student achievement on lack of parent involvement even when we have not exhausted every possibility to engage with the community on every possible occasion. Students are in school more than they are anywhere else and we often have more time with children than their parents do. We have to release these excuses from our philosophies and recognize and respect the dynamic that schools and school leadership have with the community it serves. We are in a position of both servitude and leadership, two roles in which many educators are inexperienced.

The misdeeds of our American educational history have found their way back into our present-day practice; however, there is hope to, once again, fight against that which separates us. As school counselors, we lead our schools toward becoming and remaining institutions of inclusivity, learning, and growth. As you will learn in the chapters ahead, the history of our country influences our practice but does not have to define our practice. We will invite counselors to form new habits, new thoughts, and new beliefs about education, race, and children.

Points to Consider

- Institutions throughout America are intentionally anti-racist in their approach to education.
- The history of American education is exclusive and based on white educators and white students' experiences.
- Standardized achievement theories such as those described in *The Bell Curve* are unhelpful to the populations of students served in schools.

- Culturally responsive theories of learning such as the ones described by Ladson-Billings, Holcomb-McCoy, Stephens and Lindsey, and Geneva Gay are inclusive, culturally fluent and offer avenues of achievement for all students.

References

Anderson, M. (2014, November 24). When educators understand race and racism. *Teaching Tolerance.*

Buque, M. (2017, July 19). *Deconstructing racial microaggressions within educational settings.* Session presented at the Reimagining Education Summer Institute, Columbia University, New York City, NY.

Cave, M. (Host). (2017, November 16). The desegregation of McDonogh 19: An oral history. [Radio broadcast]. In S. Holtz (Producer) *NOLA Life Stories.* New Orleans Public Radio.

D'amico, D., Pawlewicz, R. J., Earley, P. M., & McGeehan, A. P. (2017). Where are all the Black teachers? Discrimination in the teacher labor market. *Harvard Educational Review, 87*(1), 26–49.

Education Trust. (2009). *The new vision for school counselors: Scope of the work.* Washington, DC: Author.

Gay, G. (2013). Teaching to and through cultural diversity. *Curriculum Inquiry, 43,* 48–70.

Goodnow, N. (2014, October 16). "The Bell Curve" 20 years later: A Q&A with Charles Murray. *American Enterprise Institute, AEIdeas.*

Hannah-Jones, N. (2017, September 7). The resegregation of Jefferson county. *New York Times.* Retrieved from www.nytimes.com/2017/09/06/magazine/the-resegregation-of-jefferson-county.html.

Herrnstein, R. J., & Murray, C. (1994). *The bell curve: Intelligence and class structure in American Life.* New York, NY: Free Press Books.

Holcomb-McCoy, C. (1999). *Multicultural counseling training: A preliminary study.*

Holcomb-McCoy, C. (2007). *School counseling to close the achievement gap: A social justice framework for success.* Thousand Oaks, CA: Corwin SAGE.

Ladson-Billings, G. (2006). From the achievement gap to the education debt: Understanding achievement in US schools. *Educational Researcher, 35*(7), 3–12.

Lee, A. R. (Producer), & Greene, C. W. (Director). (2014). "I'm not racist … Am I?" [Motion picture]. United States: The Calhoun School and Point Made Films. Retrieved from http://notracistmovie.com.

Lemann, N. (1997, January 18). The bell curve flattened. *Slate.* Retrieved from www.theatlantic.com/past/docs/unbound/aandc/trnscrpt/lemtest.htm.

National Center for Education Statistics, U.S. Department of Education. (1993). *120 years of American education: A statistical portrait.* Washington, DC: Author.

NEA (National Education Association). (2017). *Students affected by achievement gaps.* Retrieved from www.nea.org/home/20380.htm.

Newton Public Schools. (2016). *Goals and objectives.* Retrieved from www.newton.k12.ma.us/domain/51.

Romano, J. L., Goh, M., & Wahl, K. H. (2005). School counseling in the United States: Implications for the Asia-pacific region. *Asia Pacific Education Review, 6*(2), 113–123.

Smith, P. (2017, July 19). *[Re]defining culturally relevant mentoring as part of educational leadership development.* Session presented at the Reimagining Education Summer Institute, Columbia University, New York City, NY.

Southern Education Center. (2016). *A history of private schools and race in the American South.* Atlanta, GA: Author.

Stephens, D. L., & Lindsey, R. B. (2011). *Culturally proficient collaboration: Use and misuse of school counselors.* Thousand Oaks, CA: Corwin SAGE.

Chapter 2

White Privilege
A Taboo of Advantage

Imagine two girls, Rachel (white) and Sasha (black), who grew up in subsidized housing in the Washington, DC area. Both girls have loving supportive families who hope for better things for their children. Both girls are read to, loved on, and helped through their formative years. In school, both girls work hard. Teachers quickly recognize that Rachel is "gifted" and that Sasha is a "hard worker." Undeterred by the lack of faith in her intellectual ability, Sasha continues to do well in school. Undeterred by her label as "gifted," Rachel continues to push herself to do more and more. Because Rachel is on a "gifted" course selection, she has the ability to take AP (advanced placement) and Honors courses at an earlier age, raising her GPA (grade point average) and her likelihood of getting in to the college of her choice.

Both girls go off to school, Rachel to an Ivy League university on a full academic scholarship and Sasha to a top-tier state school on a full scholarship. In the Ivy League, Rachel is accepted into the student body with ease. Others in her class find her neighborhood colloquialisms charming. In Sasha's school, people assume she may be there because of affirmative action and wonder if she has the skills needed to succeed. Others in her class find her neighborhood colloquialisms as further evidence of her lacking.

Both girls graduate from school. Rachel is able to graduate in four years due to robust paid internship opportunities awarded by alumni networks and is offered a job immediately after graduation. Sasha graduates in five years while working two jobs on the side and finds employment after a year of searching. In everyday life, Sasha has learned to dress nicely and use impeccable grammar in order to be accepted. Rachel never has to think about these things.

In this story, the pervasive effects of white privilege can be seen in each step of the way. Both girls begin at the starting point but the game is rigged. White privilege doesn't mean a group of old white men in a smoky room laughing as they cast away the dreams of minority job seekers or college hopefuls. White privilege is the advantage that we, as white people, receive because we are the majority race and have historically held positions of power within society.

Privilege can be hard to see if you are the one receiving it. Society is the giver of this privilege and therefore a white person cannot refuse to take that privilege. The privilege is embedded in every aspect of our functioning within society. There are many aspects of a person's life that can convey or not convey privilege and white privilege is one of those aspects. As such, some white people may think that they don't have privilege because they live in poverty, are not citizens of the country in which they live, or don't fluently speak the common language of where they live. However, white privilege can, and does, exist even when other areas of marginalization exist as well. Being "not-white" creates an environment where a person has to work much harder to receive the same results.

Simple examples of white privilege can be seen walking through the aisles of your local pharmacy when looking for a band-aid, hair products, or greeting cards. In my local pharmacy, the aisle contains two sides of hair products and only one small section of one shelf for non-white hair. In 2013, *The Atlantic* published "The Story of the Black Band-Aid," chronicling the creation and failing of a "black band-aid" in the late 1990s (Malo, 2013). *The Huffington Post* printed an article celebrating the fact that as of 2015, people of color could purchase bandages that matched their skin (Finley, 2015). In the article, the creator of Tru Colour Bandages, who is white and has adopted children who are black, stated:

> I just want my kids, who are already gonna struggle with the fact that they don't have the same skin color as their dad, I want them to see they were made as just as authentic and just as beautiful.
>
> (Finley, 2015, seventh paragraph)

Peggy McIntosh's quintessential article, "White Privilege: Unpacking the Invisible Knapsack," states: "I was taught to see racism only in individual acts of meanness, not in invisible systems conferring dominance on my group," and includes a checklist for understanding your level of privilege (McIntosh, 1990, p. 6).

Historical Examples

Many examples of white privilege exist in history. Often these examples are dismissed as antiquated and no longer relevant, but the opposite is true. One example of a racist practice that has lasting effects is redlining. Redlining began during the depression when many homeowners were at risk of losing their homes. Trying to stem the tide of foreclosures, the government sponsored the Home Owners Loan Corporation (HOLC). Part of the work of the HOLC was to survey neighborhoods and grade each neighborhood according to a series of criteria. Most of the neighborhoods designated in red and deemed "hazardous" were designated with the note "Infiltration of: Negroes." In fact, a neighborhood with just one person of color living in it merited this distinction. Visit the University of Richmond's interactive *Mapping Inequality* website to see more about redlining in your area (University of Richmond Digital Scholarship Lab, 2018).

The Fair Housing Act (FH Act), title VIII of the Civil Rights Act of 1968, makes these practices illegal. In spite of this, the Department of Housing and Urban Development still actively investigates redlining cases annually, including a $200 million settlement with Associated Bank, N.A. in 2015. Even when banks are willing to lend to residents of redlined neighborhoods and applicants of color, the lack of home ownership in the history of a family may contribute to a lack of family wealth for down payment for a home today. Jamelle Bouie does a great job describing this effect in *How We Built the Ghettos* by saying: "when you prevent a whole class of people from building wealth, accessing capital, or leaving impoverished areas, you guarantee cultural dysfunction and deep, generational poverty. When it comes to inner-city poverty—we built that" (Bouie, 2014, final para.).

Not only does historic redlining affect the ability of people of color to afford to buy a house, it affects the housing prices in historically black neighborhoods and communities. In a recent Boston College study, housing prices from 1990 were approximately 5 percent lower for homes within redlined communities, resulting in a value decrease of $7,500 even 22 years after redlining was made illegal (Appel & Nickerson, 2016).

Contemporary Examples

Besides everyday examples of white privilege in band-aid colors and hair products, being a white person can give the privilege of career options and optimal medical care. In a widely known 2004 Harvard study, resumés with white-sounding names were 50 percent more likely to receive callbacks for interviews (Bertrand & Mullainathan, 2004).

Racial disparities in treatment do not only affect adults, children are also affected by white privilege. A study conducted at Stanford found that teachers were significantly more likely to identify a black student as a "troublemaker" after a second infraction than a white student (Okonofua & Eberhardt, 2015). This bias may be one part of the racial disparities we see in suspensions and expulsions in our schools. Racial disparities are also seen in the likelihood of patients to receive pain medication in treatment. In children diagnosed with appendicitis and in severe pain, black children were significantly less likely to be given pain medication (Goyal, Kuppermann, Cleary, Teach, & Chamberlain, 2015). It is our assertion that teachers and medical providers care for their patients and want what is best for them, but biases and cultural influences affect practitioners in ways they may be unaware of.

So Now What?

White privilege is pervasive, sneaky, and embedded in who we are. If we neglect to talk about it and hide beneath our cloak of "color blind" then we will lose the opportunity to be a part of the change. To put it succinctly:

> If we don't talk about white privilege, we are complicit in the existence and perpetuation of the privilege given to those who are white and are actively counteracting the belief that all humans are equal.

Let's take a moment to define counteract: act against something to reduce its force or neutralize it. If we do not talk about white privilege and are complicit in the privilege given to those who are white, we are *acting against* the belief that all humans are equal.

This is hard work. White people, particularly, can feel very uncomfortable talking about race. In the book *NurtureShock*, the authors explore this issue in a chapter titled "Why White Parents Don't Talk About Race" (Bronson &

Merryman, 2009). In one instance, white parents were so uncomfortable talking about race that they dropped out of a study when they learned that honest conversations about race would be a part of the expectations. In another instance, children were overheard saying: "parents don't like us to talk about our skin, so don't let them hear you" (Bronson & Merryman, 2009, p. 56).

In reality, race is a fundamental part of our identities and deserves to be acknowledged and appreciated. In a country whose history is so embedded in racial inequalities, race is a part of who we are. Race is not taboo, not a secret, not something to be whispered about amongst your friends. Acknowledging race is only part of the solution. Because we have experienced centuries of skin color-based treatment, we function as if race is a fact. Race is limiting, created without much biological science, but we behave as if it is real and meaningful. Conversely, we are not "color blind" in the sense that we are unable to identify tan skin from dark brown skin. We see skin color but we can undo negative implications of the social construct. It is here that the work begins.

The Work for School Counselors

As school counselors, we must work within the ethical guidelines of our field. In the American School Counselor Association (ASCA) *Ethical Standards for School Counselors*, cultural sensitivity is defined as:

> a set of skills enabling you to know, understand and value the similarities and differences in people and modify your behavior to be most effective and respectful of students and families and to deliver programs that fit the needs of diverse learners.
>
> (ASCA, 2016, p. 9)

Cultural competencies are referenced 11 times within the 12-page document.

In order to create a school counseling program and school that fits the needs of diverse learners, work will need to take place to combat white privilege within your building and community. Increasing access for students to privileged spaces without making it a safe space is not enough. As educators, and adults, we cannot let the work of breaking down privilege fall solely on the shoulders of our children.

A safe and collaborative environment for discussion is going to be integral to this work. However, that doesn't mean that all conversations about race and privilege will be comfortable. Think about the last time that you learned a new skill, you were likely frustrated at times, excited at times, angry at times, and may have wanted to give up. Expect all of these and more when working on creating an equitable school environment.

I've often joked that if it's uncomfortable, ask the school counselor. Think of all the times that you have worked with a student or group of students when others felt squeamish or unsure what to do. Perhaps this is why school counselors are uniquely qualified to begin the work of systemic change for equity. Counselors have the leadership, advocacy, and collaboration skills needed, plus the ability to work within discomfort for change.

Create a Safe, Collaborative Environment

Like many things in a school, the work begins with the staff. Take the time to assess the climate of the staff before beginning equity conversations in your building. Do staff members feel safe asking questions and sharing opinions that may differ from other staff members? Do they feel safe asking questions and sharing opinions that differ from administration? I once worked in a building where everything said would likely be reported to the administrator who would call staff into her office to follow up. Staff members lived in fear that they would say the wrong thing and be reprimanded. Honest, open conversations about equity would not have been possible in this environment.

If you determine that the school needs to build a more safe, collaborative environment, *stop there*. In this case, slowing down and building a strong foundation of trust within your school will result in better results for your work later. While we can feel excited to move forward, this foundation is crucial.

Once your staff can work together in a trusting environment, consider the other stakeholders in your school community. Do students have a safe and trusting environment in which to share their thoughts and ideas with teachers? With each other? How is communication with parents? We are talking about changing the entire way we see the world, the people in it, and how we move through our system. Trust is paramount for everyone.

In building trust, it can be helpful to access the affective as a first step. In Chapter 6, we include specific activities that you can use. The affective refers to our feelings or moods. When we have discussions about white privilege, race, and equity, we may tend to speak only intellectually or go straight to negative feelings that we bring into the conversations. To increase the collaboration amongst the group, begin with topics that are less difficult and access positive feelings. For instance, start a discussion with what you ate for dinner last night, watched on TV, or a vacation you would like to take. After accessing this positive feeling, the group can move to a slightly more intense topic. The positive feelings will "carry over" in the conversation and help the group to be more open to new ideas.

Of course, this technique is ineffective in environments where people are wary or unsure of the climate. School counselors can support those who are reticent by asking what they are thinking or feeling rather than expressing expectations. Again, this is an area where school counselors bring a unique skill set to manage group dynamics and scaffold participation for effective conversations.

Notice White Privilege

It is said that the first step is acknowledging you have a problem. Begin the work of noticing white privilege in your building by disaggregating data. Data is a solid place to start if you are still building buy-in within your staff or school leadership for the work of equity. Numbers can seem less judgemental or subjective, allowing for more open conversation.

Questions You Might Investigate:

- Do students of color have more office referrals than their white peers?
- Are students of color more likely to be suspended?
- Are students of color more likely to be recommended for advanced placement or honors courses?
- Do white students receive more waivers for honors placement when their data does not meet requirements?
- Are white students more likely to be on cohort for graduation?
- Do students of color have more absences than their white peers?
- Are students of color more likely to express disenfranchisement on climate surveys?
- Are students of color less likely to have a strong connection with at least one staff member?
- What is your achievement gap?
- Are non-white students more likely to be referred for special education students without intense intervention?
- Are there any areas where gaps between white students and students of color are smaller or nonexistent?

The American School Counselor Association has a useful "School Data Profile" (ASCA, n.d.) spreadsheet tool that school counselors can use as a starting point for digging deeper into data using an equity lens.

Caution: Avoid jumping straight from data to strategies, doing so might overlook the reality of your student's experiences. Take the time to create a complex picture of what's working and what's not. If your school has areas where data indicates that gaps are smaller or nonexistent between white and non-white students, pay special attention to the possible causes for this positive indicator. Build on what's working while tearing down what is not.

Once the school begins to look at data with a critical eye, encourage staff members to pay attention in the halls, cafeterias, and other areas of the building. Remembering that white privilege is pervasive and sneaky, acknowledge that privilege may be ingrained in the culture of the school.

Caution: Begin with noticing in a non-judgemental way. Buy-in will not increase with the feeling that the white-privilege police are questioning everything that anyone does. Encourage sharing of times that staff members (or students) see white privilege while not calling out specific people. It can also be helpful for school counselors to acknowledge times that they have noticed white privilege at work in their own interactions with others. This is possible even for school counselors of color. After all, we are all members of a society where white privilege is a part of every aspect of our world.

Questions You Might Investigate:

- Are non-white students more likely to be stopped when walking in the hallway and questioned about their purpose or for a hall pass?
- Are white students more likely to receive a warning for the same behavior that might result in a consequence or even suspension for a non-white student?

- Are students of color more likely to be asked to be quiet?
- Do teachers act surprised or overly proud when a non-white student answers a question correctly?
- Are teachers more likely to select white students to answer questions?

Take a look at your Parent Teacher Association (PTA), do the members of the PTA represent the diversity of your building? I used to work in a school that was over 80 percent minority students. For many years, our PTA was approximately 95 percent white. While the PTA members were wonderful, hard working parents who cared about our school, I look back and think of what a missed opportunity we had.

Questions You Might Investigate:

- What is the racial makeup of your PTA and of your student body?
- What is the racial makeup of your PTA leadership and your student body or the PTA itself?
- Have any non-white parents been personally invited to join the PTA?
- What barriers exist for parent participation in the PTA?
- What is the perspective of the current PTA leadership on implementing new ideas to increase diversity?

Take a look at your staff, do members of your staff represent the diversity of your student body? Administrators will tell you that they have far fewer non-white applicants for teaching positions than white applicants. In a July 2016 report, the U.S. Department of Education reported that in 2012–13, only 25 percent of education majors were non-white (U.S. Department of Education, 2016). The work to increase minority education majors is outside the scope of the work of one school counseling program. However, efforts to increase the number of teachers of color in your building are possible.

Questions You Might Investigate:

- What percentage of interviews are white applicants?
- What percentage of hires are white applicants?
- How does the retention rate differ for white teachers and teachers of color?

Finally, noticing white privilege means listening to your gut. If something feels not-quite-right, it probably isn't. One of the easiest gut checks is to ask, would we do the same if this student/parent/staff were white? Or, conversely, would we do the same if this student/parent/staff were not white?

Call It Out When You See It

Once you've established a safe, collaborative environment with your staff, students, and parents, and begun noticing white privilege when it's happening, it's time to call it when you see it. This is hard. It's uncomfortable. It's time to speak even when your voice shakes.

Who Should Speak Up?

Everyone. Even more if you are white. It's time to dispel the polite society that privilege has created. In "Cracking the Codes: The System of Racial Inequity," a film from World Trust, Joy DeGruy shares a story about a trip to a grocery store where her sister-in-law used her white privilege to speak up when she notices Joy being treated differently because she is black (Butler, 2000). Joy states: "she walked through the world differently than I did." If being white gives privilege, it makes sense that the privilege be used to increase social justice. Being an ally for racial equity is a verb and not an identity. Allyship is an active process taken on by people who are not marginalized in the same way by our society.

But, How?

Be curious. Rather than calling people out in a way intended to shame them, ask questions in a way that involves self-reflective and critical thinking. Use phrases like "I'm wondering," "Did you notice," and "What if." When speaking with students, be particularly cautious in allowing the space to learn and grow without shaming. If this is hard work for adults, it's even harder for children. We have been socialized to be polite and not to make rude comments to others. Sometimes, it might feel rude to call someone out for a racist or privileged comment. It's helpful to think that rising to meet a rude comment is not rude, it is positive. Sometimes, the person may be a "would-be ally," they want to do the right thing and will accept and learn from your interruption. Other times, the person might be embarrassed and change the subject. Either way, you send a message that this is not acceptable and you can show your allyship.

Systems Change is Systemic Change

Working against white privilege doesn't only mean reaction. Talk about white privilege even when you don't see it. Hold discussions in staff meetings, classrooms, and parent gatherings about race and equality. In the report, *Systems Change: A Guide to What It Is and How to do It*, the authors define systems change as "an intentional process designed to alter the status quo by shifting the function or structure of an identified system with purposeful interventions" (Abercrombie, Harries, & Wharton, 2015, p. 9). Systems change might include routines, relationships, resources, and policies within your building. As school counselors, we are charged with systemic change that allows all students equitable access to education and postsecondary options of their choosing.

So what are the boundaries of the system? For our purpose, we are looking at the school staff, parents, and students. While many outside factors influence the work within your building, this may fall outside the realm of the school counselor and their immediate work. Many proactive school counselors work with their school boards, communities, and other outside stakeholders for the good of their students. If you are comfortable doing so, continue your advocacy!

School counselors are practitioners who work within the system they are working to change. Counselors will need to strategize the efforts that they make on behalf of systemic change and the efforts they make on behalf of specific students. In addition, it is necessary for the school counselor to work within the parameters of their role and job position while utilizing their skills for leadership, advocacy, and collaboration. After all, systemic change is not possible if the counselor is out of a job.

Looking at areas of systemic change other than race and equity might be helpful to see patterns of strengths and strategies that were successful. In the past, women were relegated to secretarial jobs or staying home with their children. As a society, we increased the opportunities for women not only by combating sexism when it arises but by teaching girls that they can be an astronaut, the president, or an engineer, and purposefully reviewing systems that led to an under-representation of women in STEM careers. To apply this strategy to racial equity, incorporate people's race into conversation with students to show that race isn't a secret or a taboo. Talk honestly about the difficulties that people of different races experience in the world. Read books that not only talk about race but also books that incorporate non-white characters and their experiences without necessarily being about race. In Chapter 5, we include lessons and activities to use with students of all ages. Finally, review systems that lead to an under-representation of students of color in honors courses and student leadership opportunities.

Anti-bullying efforts can also show patterns of strengths and strategies that are successful. Anti-bullying efforts are now a part of state laws, school district policies, and everyday functioning of schools. In a 2011 report, the Department of Education pinpointed the 1999 Columbine High School shooting as the first of many incidents of school violence tied to bullying as an underlying cause (U.S. Department of Education, 2011). This high-profile case sparked national interest in anti-bullying efforts. Similarly, many high-profile incidents of racial inequity have occurred in recent years. School counselors can use this intensified focus on racial equity as their platform for work within the school. In Chapter 6, we include activities to use with staff members to increase focus and awareness on racial inequities in your school.

Of course, each of these examples is vastly more complicated than can be summarized in a brief paragraph. Social change will require action at many levels and what worked in one area of system change will not always work for another. We encourage counselors to look at what has worked in their community and their schools to lead change for the better and use these tools in their own work for equity.

What If People Don't Like It?

Let's face it, people don't like being told they are wrong. When you push back, question what is happening, and call out white privilege, you are likely to ruffle a few feathers. This can be extremely uncomfortable for anyone, but as school counselors we must also maintain a positive relationship with our students, teachers, and parents so that we can continue to interact collaboratively. In Chapter 10, we will discuss criticism and push-back more broadly in terms of equity and social justice. Here, we will explore how to get started on the one concept of white privilege.

Find (or Create) Your Advocates

Before you begin systematic efforts to increase equality and interrupt white privilege in your school, gain the support of your building administration. While individuals can work to interrupt privilege in isolation, administrator support will be crucial to any school-wide efforts. Think about what is important to your administrator and look at your school improvement plan. Come to your principal with the compelling reason for your idea. If your principal is concerned about test scores, show them how you could decrease the achievement gap, causing the overall passing rate to increase. If your principal is concerned about parent perception of the school, show them how you could increase parent engagement. Principals work hard to have a vision for their building and deal with many outside pressures to perform. If we want our work to rise to the top of the school's to-do list, we must present the work in a way that matches the compelling why of the school's leadership.

Once you have the support of administration, find your other advocates in your building. Do you have teachers or staff members that you know are active in social justice in the community? Are open to new ideas? Invite them to talk with you about your ideas for interrupting privilege and spread the word of change. Look at your student body and find students who are active and work for equality. Even in elementary school, students can be a part of a leadership club that takes on social justice issues at an age-appropriate level. Are there parents who might be willing to support your efforts at the systems change level by taking on some responsibilities for processes that are changing due to the work of interrupting privilege. For instance, if your PTA does not reflect the diversity of your student body, you might ask parents to call and personally invite new members to the next PTA meeting.

Encourage Growth Mindset

Carol Dweck's "Theory of Growth" mindset has gained popularity but can often be misunderstood (Mindset Works Inc., 2017). Growth mindset is the idea that effort or training can change one's ability. In discussions about race, there is a tendency to fall into the idea that good people are not prejudiced. In reality, all people who live in a society so embedded in white privilege are affected by their environment and will need to continuously work for change. In a 2011 TEDx talk, Jay Smooth discussed the idea that race is a social construct that was "shaped specifically to rationalize and justify indefensible acts. When we grapple with race issues, we grapple with something designed for centuries to make us circumvent our best instincts" (TEDx Hampshire College, 2011). It is no surprise that this is hard work. We will all make mistakes. In order to create change in your school while maintaining a positive relationship with students, teachers, and parents, it will be necessary to continuously incorporate the idea that this is ongoing work rather than a task to complete. Start with being honest and sharing the mistakes that you have made.

Create New Stories

When interrupting white privilege, you will often hear stories in return. Stories about why this isn't actually white privilege or why this white person isn't privileged. Stories about why we've always done it this way. Stories about how we can't help the rules, we just apply them.

Early in my career, the district where I worked implemented a new procedure for identifying students who would be placed in honors math courses. Previously, the decision had been made by teachers at the end of the school year. When looking at honors enrollment, the district identified a large number of students of color who were not in honors courses in spite of performing successfully in the previous year. In the new procedure, counselors would identify several data points and place students according to set criteria. Teachers were able to apply for a waiver to place a student into honors but were not permitted to "waiver down." The district tested in several pilot schools and found that the rate of students succeeding in honors classes increased as a result of this effort.

When my school implemented the new criteria, I had many teachers ask what they should do if they felt a student wouldn't be successful. One teacher asked me: "aren't we just setting him up for failure?" I believe that this teacher wanted what was best for her student and had created a story where she was worried that her student wouldn't succeed, in spite of the fact that several years of data suggested he had the skills necessary to do well in honors. I gently supported the creation of a new story—one where the student had shown over the past few years that he was successful in learning new math concepts and that being enrolled in honors math would allow him to continue this success, and that future teachers would scaffold, differentiate, and support as needed just as this teacher had done. Imagine if I had said: "you just think that because he's black." The conversation would have ended there and the teacher would have been unwilling or unable to discuss the idea further.

Make a Plan for the Big Stuff

Privilege and power can't be negated by simply stating it is there. If you see systemic issues within your school or district, find your allies within your building and make a plan to combat while relating to the compelling why of the school. Incorporate interrupting privilege into the everyday work of the building. We talk more about using data in Chapter 9, but for the purposes of this chapter we will look at one example.

In an elementary school where I worked, we noticed that achievement gap between white students and students of color broadened over their time at the school. In kindergarten, the gap was very small and each year it grew bigger. Rather than believing the story that the decline had to do with poverty, family values, or other euphemisms of white privilege, we dug deeper to determine ways to combat our achievement gap. In reality, many racial issues embedded in our society were likely at play, but, for our building, our students, we were going to make a change regardless of the role of the world outside our doors. We created a new system where we monitored student growth more closely and responded early so that students did not fall behind a little each year and reach fifth grade not ready for transition to middle school. We worked together to individualize instruction as much as possible so that all students were receiving what they needed. We did not erase our achievement gap, and we had much more work we could have been doing, but we did decrease the widening of the gap from kindergarten to fifth grade.

What Will You Have to Give Up?

Systemic work means change and change is hard. When we work to change the entire culture of our building in contradiction of our dominant culture, we will have to give up some things that we may hold dear. The first step is giving up the idea that your school is doing its best now. This is no small ask. When teachers and staff members are working hard every day, literally through blood, sweat, and tears, it is a lot to say "this is not enough."

Your building may also have to give up traditions or customs that it currently values. For instance, a family history activity may be difficult for students whose family records may be left incomplete due to slavery and Jim Crow laws. I stuck my foot in my mouth once when I glibly told a class of mostly African American and Hispanic students that "all families" have a family crest. Of course, this is not the case at all. I still taught the family crest activity, but I added a lesson teaching of medieval customs and incorporated other ideas of family customs.

Some people may not be ready to confront their own role in privilege in your building. We have some ideas to help you in Chapter 10, but know now that you, as the school counselor, may have to give up the idea that you will be liked by everyone you work with. As school counselors, we must maintain positive working relationships with everyone and we want to help you to stand up for racial equity in a respectful, collaborative way, but you may lose friends. Is that OK with you? Are you ready to take on this work?

Points to Consider

- Society is the giver of white privilege, white people cannot refuse to accept the privilege.
- White privilege is embedded in history and its effects still impact people of color today.
- If we don't talk about white privilege, we are complicit in its perpetuation.
- Increasing access to places of privilege must be combined with creating a safe place.
- Use data to mine for privilege.
- Speak up, especially if you are white.
- Start in your building and be prepared to give up traditions, customs, and procedures.

References

Abercrombie, R., Harries, E., & Wharton, R. (2015). *Systems change: A guide to what it is and how to do it.* London: New Philanthropy Capital.

Appel, I., & Nickerson, J. (2016). *Pockets of poverty: The long-term effects of redlining.* Available from SSRN: https://ssrn.com/abstract=2852856 or http://dx.doi.org/10.2139/ssrn.2852856.

ASCA (American School Counselor Association). *School Data Profile*. Available from: www. schoolcounselor.org/asca/media/asca/ASCA%20National%20Model%20Templates/School-DataProfile.xls.

ASCA (American School Counselor Association). (2016). *ASCA ethical standards for school counselors*. Alexandria, VA: Author.

Bertrand, M., & Mullainathan, S. (2004). Are Emily and Greg more employable than Lakisha and Jamal? A field experiment on labor market discrimination. *American Economic Review, 94*(4), 991–1013.

Bouie, J. (2014, March 13). How we built the ghettos. *The Daily Beast*. Retrieved from www. thedailybeast.com/how-we-built-the-ghettos.

Bronson, P., & Merryman, A. (2009). *Nurtureshock: New thinking about children*. Lebanon, IN: Twelve Books, Hatchette Book Group.

Butler, S. (Producer, Director), & Butler, R. (Director). "Cracking the codes: The system of racial inequality." [Motion picture]. Available from World Trust Educational Services, 2000 Franklin St., 3rd Floor, Oakland, CA, 94612.

Fair Housing Act of 1968, 42 U.S.C. §§3601–3631 (2018).

Finley, T. (2015, October 7). People of color can finally wear bandages that match their skin. *The Huffington Post*. Retrieved from www.huffingtonpost.com/entry/people-of-color-can-finally-wear-bandages-that-match-their-skin_us_56155977e4b0fad1591a6845.

Goyal, M. K., Kuppermann, N., Cleary, S. D., Teach, S. J., & Chamberlain, J. M. (2015). Racial disparities in pain management of children with appendicitis in emergency departments. *JAMA Pediatrics, 169*, 996–1002.

Malo, S. (2013, June 6). The story of the black band-aid. *The Atlantic*. Retrieved from www. theatlantic.com/health/archive/2013/06/the-story-of-the-black-band-aid/276542/.

McIntosh, P. (1990, Winter). White privilege: Unpacking the invisible knapsack. *Independent School* [Excerpt].

Mindset Works, Inc. (2017). *Decades of scientific research that started a growth mindset revolution.*

Okonofua, J. A., & Eberhardt, J. L. (2015). Two strikes: Race and the disciplining of young students. *Psychological Science, 26*, 617–624.

TEDx Hampshire College. (2011, November 15). "Jay Smooth—How I learned to stop worrying and love discussing race." [Video file].

University of Richmond Digital Scholarship Lab. (2018). [Interactive map of the United States outlining the process of redlining from 1935–40]. *Mapping Inequality*.

U.S. Department of Education, Office of Planning, Evaluation and Policy Development, Policy and Program Studies Service. (2011, December). *Analysis of state bullying laws and policies*. Washington, DC: Author.

U.S. Department of Education, Office of Planning, Evaluation and Policy Development, Policy and Program Studies Service. (2016, July). *The state of racial diversity in the educator workforce*. Washington, DC: Author.

Chapter 3

Implicit Bias

A Disconnect Between Intention and Outcome

We believe that the vast majority of teachers, counselors, administrators, and school personnel want what is best for all students. They work tirelessly, every single day, to help students to achieve their dreams for the future. If this is the case, why do we have a gap in achievement between white students and students of color? There is a disconnect between the intention of the educator and the outcome for student. The achievement gap is evident across the country and in all types of school settings.

In Chapter 1, we looked at the history of the achievement gap, beginning with desegregation and continuing to the current day, based on the idea of standardized achievement. In the last chapter, we explored how white privilege is embedded within the systems of the United States. Historically, systems were created for whites only and purposefully marginalized people of color, creating a system of white privilege. We must constantly interrupt privilege in order to counteract its unearned advantage. Because we all live within this system of white privilege, watch TV that perpetuates white privilege, see ads that constantly remind us that white people are the most beautiful and enviable, and see the values of the white culture held above all others, we all have a bias against people of color.

Wait a minute, you say, I am not biased against people of color. I have many friends, family members even, who are people of color. You might be saying, I am not biased against people of color—I am a person of color! Bias can exist whether you consciously agree with it. Let's explore how implicit bias works both generally and in relation to race. Humans are conditioned to respond to patterns within our world. There is an evolutionary advantage to fast, automatic responses based on patterns or associations. You see a long, thin object moving along, you don't stop to determine if it's a snake or a rope—you jump out of the way. In this context, we can see that implicit is a fast, automatic response that does not rely on thought or deliberation. We are not always aware of the implicit reactions that we have until after they have happened.

When making decisions in everyday life, our brains often rely on automatic responses. Get in the car, and your hand will reach for the seat belt. Have you ever tried to teach a child to tie their shoes? After years of tying your own shoes, it's hard to explain the explicit, deliberate process to someone else. The tricky part is that we often use our explicit, cognitive thought processes to explain away our implicit, automatic responses. The guy that was walking down the street, did he actually show signs of being dangerous or was your automatic bias taking effect? For example, when working with people who live in poverty, you might overhear a lot of judgements of that person's work ethic, priorities, or mental health. What starts as an implicit bias (poor people are less than wealthier or middle-class people) turns into an explicit cognitive response (there is a reason "these people" are poor).

Implicit bias is judgement or bias based in subtle cognitive processes. Because implicit bias happens so subtly, it affects our behavior and choices in ways that we may not notice. In education, we have a divide between what we intend and the actions we take. The achievement gap is a result of this divide. In order to change our actions, we must break the habit of implicit bias by shining a light on the subtle cognitive processes that lead to inequity. While inequity happens in many domains, we will focus here on racial inequities perpetuated by racism.

Stop here, you might say, I am not racist and neither are my colleagues. Here's the truth—racism is not just about saying you dislike people of other races, or that you think that black people shouldn't have the same rights that white people have. I hope, especially if you are in education, that is not your belief system. Racism has much deeper roots. In the article *Sociology of Racism* from Harvard researcher Matthew Clair and Canadian scholar Jeffrey Denis, racism is defined as "an ideology of racial domination in which the presumed biological or cultural superiority of one or more racial groups is used to justify or prescribe the inferior treatment or social positions of other groups" (Clair & Denis, 2015, p.857).

In education, students of color achieve at significantly lower rates than white students. When asked why that is, you might hear about parent involvement, poverty, attitude about education, or many other factors that presume superiority of the mainstream white culture to justify that lower achievement rate. However, the 2013 National Assessment of Educational Progress project found that the average reading score for eighth grade black students from middle-class households is the same as white students from households eligible for free and reduced lunch (U.S. Department of Education, 2013). Seventy-eight percent of African American people in the United States do not live in poverty (Kaiser Family Foundation, 2017). Even though the vast majority of African American friends, students, and colleagues are not living in poverty, there is often a false association between poverty and being black. When we reflect our beliefs about lower achievement, we may realize there are assumptions made that are not factual or supported by the data. We would prefer, perhaps, to blame socioeconomic status on achievement but, in reality, achievement is not accessible to black students the way it is for white students, regardless of economics, involvement, or attitudes.

The implicit reactions of our brain rely on patterns and associations. As adults who grew up in inequitable schools, live in inequitable communities, and work in inequitable environments, we see the pattern of students of color performing below grade- level and this increases our likelihood of perpetuating our racial bias and, thus, systemic racism. This phenomenon is called confirmation bias, defined as "the seeking or interpreting of evidence in ways that are partial to existing beliefs, expectations, or a hypothesis in hand" (Nickerson, 1998, p. 175).

In a report from the Economic Policy Institute, researchers found that attending a high-poverty school lowers math and reading proficiency in all racial subgroups but that poor white children are significantly less likely than black students to attend a high-poverty school (Carnoy & Garcia, 2017). According to the

National Equity Atlas, a joint data project run by PolicyLink and the University of Southern California, 76.9 percent of black students attended a high-poverty school (over 50 percent free and reduced lunch) in 2014. Because a high-poverty school is less likely to have high performing students and is more likely to have students of color, the system itself not only allows black students to be disproportionately disadvantaged but supports a confirmation bias that black students are less likely to achieve than white students.

We must *interrupt racism* when we see it in others, in our schools, and within ourselves. We have explored that disparities exist between white students and students of color within the system of education. Take the time to look at the achievement of students by racial subgroup within your school. Don't just look at passing rates for standardized tests. Take the time to look at universal screening tools like Dynamic Indicators of Basic Early Literacy Skills (DIBELS) or mCLASS. Look at the disparity between white students and students of color in Advanced Placement or honors enrollment or Academically and Intellectually Gifted (AIG) identification. We will talk more about utilizing data for systemic change in Chapter 9. Do you see that disparities exist in your school?

If disparities exist in your school, do they exist in each classroom? For each grade level? In your counseling program? It gets harder and harder to "own" the disparities as they become more and more connected to our own work. We are all here because we care about kids. We *want* to do the right thing. We don't want to have to say that we're not serving our students.

When confronted with the idea that we might have bias or we might be perpetuating racism, it's easy to use the explicit side of our brain to explain away the disparity.

I was recently discussing racial disparities with a group of colleagues. One of the school counselors works at a school in which the majority of students live in poverty and are of color. Their test scores are well below the average of the district as a whole. She asked: "Are there things that we are doing within our building that are keeping our students from doing well because of our own privilege?" I could see the hurt in her face; I know that she cares deeply about doing right by her students. It might be easy to give a reassuring answer but, by doing so, we miss the opportunity to create change for the better. Instead, I asked her to go back to her school and look at the percentage of students on grade level at the end of each grade, disaggregated by race. It's typical to see that the percentage of Kindergarteners on grade level is higher than the percentage of fifth graders who are. If you disaggregate by race, do you see a widening gap between white students and students of color? If so, it is likely that factors within your building are disproportionately favoring or supporting white students.

What arguments do you hear in the breakroom or planning times about why groups of students aren't succeeding? I was once in a leadership team meeting where we were looking at our achievement gap. This was my first year in the school, and I was appalled. How could a school of such hard working teachers not be reaching every student? I knew that the teachers within my building were trying, but clearly something was amiss. The principal quickly dismissed the achievement gap as caused by poverty, or a variety of other excuses. It was hard to offer critique in a new building, with a new boss, and new colleagues. It took a lot of courage to stand up and say that I didn't think we could dismiss such a large achievement gap without digging deeper to find root causes. In retrospect, I wish I had done more to use data to support systemic change within that school.

Implications

We have explored the history of the achievement gap, the power of white privilege, and the pervasive effects of implicit bias. What are our next steps? The first step is to acknowledge that every person has implicit biases and biases related to race. This isn't a judgement against those with biases. It's a natural part of the way our brains work and we are a product of the society that we live in. We are all affected.

One of the constant struggles of equity work is the feeling that we are stuck. The system is set up to disadvantage people of color. In fact, the education system was created only for white people and hasn't drastically changed over the years. In this chapter, we have good news. Implicit bias can be changed. Because it is a habit of the mind, we can create a new habit by interrupting the racial bias over and over to create new habits and new automaticity. If we stay in the zone where we are stuck, change will never happen. Implicit bias is a great place to start for yourself and your staff, students, and parents.

A body of research exists in so called "shooter-bias" studies where participants are asked to decide whether to shoot a pretend gun in response to white or non-white targets in a video game. Historically, participants are faster to shoot an armed target when they are black, and more likely to make an error and shoot an unarmed target when they are black. In a 2013 study, researchers looked at the effects training and expertise may have in reducing racial bias in the decision to shoot. In the first experiment, novices read a newspaper article about black criminals and were then more likely to show racial bias in the shooter task. When novices read about white criminals, the bias was eliminated, indicating that they were more likely to shoot armed white targets, thus eliminating the racial gap (Sims, Correll, & Sadler, 2013). Police officers were unaffected by the same stereotype manipulation. The authors theorized that police officers were better trained in identifying armed targets and were less likely to be easily biased. Recent high-profile police shootings of unarmed black people contradicts this. More research in this area is necessary to fully understand the effects of training on bias.

In experiment 2, novice participants were "trained" that armed targets were more likely to be black by increasing the base rates of black armed target in repeated shooting tasks. This means that at the beginning of the game, black targets were the most likely to be armed (Sims et al., 2013). Likewise, in experiment 3, the authors studied police officers who were routinely dealing with minority gang members and thus "trained" to relate armed targets with racial bias. In comparing experiments 2 and 3, both novices and police officers could be biased. The training itself reinforced the association between blacks and danger. The authors state "in a sense, when race becomes a task-relevant cue, even experts may rely on it to facilitate weapon detection" (Sims et al., 2013, p. 300).

So how does this relate to your school building? Think about the connection of race and performance. When a teacher, counselor or staff member sees over and over that students of color are more likely to be poor or to perform below grade level, the race of the student can become a task-relevant cue. Educators are experts on learning and instruction just as police officers are experts in weapon detection. However, even the experts can be impacted by bias and stereotypes. When an educator makes an assumption that a student is below grade level or needs additional support, they may be less likely to offer that child access to rigor or to push the child outside of their comfort zone in learning. I was recently speaking with a teacher friend who has a Latino child in her class. It was close to the beginning of the school year so the teacher didn't know her students very well yet. She shared that a well meaning staff member wanted to include this Latino student in a food drive that was happening at the school. My friend stated that she was confused because "I'm pretty sure her dad is a doctor." The staff member had made an assumption related to her bias that Latino students are more likely to be poor and to need more support. I have also been impacted by my own bias. When working at a high-needs magnet school, most of our white students were magnet students (thus coming from wealthier neighborhoods) and most of our black students were "base" students (coming from the poor neighborhoods surrounding the school). This was a fact and was supported by our demographic data. However, my own thinking was trained to assume that white students were affluent and black students were poor. Of course, this was not always true and my own bias affected my ability to determine the needs of students individually.

Talking about bias is uncomfortable. Adults typically shy away from talking about bias because they are worried that they may look insensitive or be accused of being racist. I recently attended a workshop on equity and bias. In the session, the presenter showed a picture of a woman wearing a hijab and asked us to share our thoughts when we saw the picture. He wanted us to be honest and "turn off our filter." I shared that I was often surprised when I saw a white woman wearing a hijab as the woman in the photo appeared white to me. Of course, we don't know what racial identity she has. Another participant in the meeting immediately jumped up and nearly shouted at me that I didn't know that the woman in the picture was white. I felt deeply uncomfortable and shut down for the rest of the conversation. As a person who actively engages in discussions about race, I was scared to say the wrong thing. Think about your staff and what you think their worries and concerns might be in discussing bias. How can we re-teach bad habits and learn new ways if we don't actively work on bias as a professional?

We see the effects of bias when looking at the phenomena of opportunity hoarding. As the name suggests, opportunity hoarding indicates the tendency of the white and affluent to restrict access to resources. The phrase was originally coined by Charles Tilley in 1998 to describe the tendency to restrict access to resources by other groups of people (Rury & Saatcioglu, 2015). In schools, this can be seen in the allocation of funding through property taxes. More affluent school districts have access to greater funding. Even in larger districts that encompass high- and low-income areas and spread resources among them, opportunity hoarding still occurs through PTAs and non-profit foundations to supplement the school budget.

Opportunity hoarding can also be seen within school buildings. Are there services or activities that are available on a "first come, first served" basis, or after school hours? Does this negatively affect certain specific groups within your building? I was recently speaking with a teacher who was telling me about a student of color in her class who was performing three grades above grade level. I asked if this student was in AIG (academically and intellectually gifted) and she stated he was not. In past years, the AIG teacher sent home paperwork for the parent to sign, but the child never gave the paper to their parent, therefore the child was not tested even though it seems evident that his needs would be best met through AIG support. The opportunity for AIG was reserved for those who actively sought it out and not based on specific criteria or by student need. In addition, we see the bias of the school. If a white student were three grade levels above average, I do not think it likely that they would be passed over for AIG. Fast forward a few years and this student is completely disengaged from school and parents and the school think that he is depressed. His current teacher is working tirelessly to find both counseling and academic enrichment for him. But what would have happened to this child if his current teacher had not advocated for him?

Personal Reflection

You may be thinking about the role that biases play in your decision making for students. If there is an achievement gap in your school, there is an achievement gap in your classrooms, and there is an achievement gap in your school counseling program unless you are actively working against the bias and privilege that our entire culture operates within.

We have included many personal reflection activities for you in Chapter 4. Consider taking the Implicit Association Test (IAT; available online at www. implicit.harvard.edu (Implicit Association Test Corporation, n.d.)). The IAT asks participants to pair two concepts; the more you implicitly associate these two concepts, the more quickly you can pair them together. If the pair goes against your implicit association (e.g. good and elderly), you pair them together much more slowly because your explicit brain is now having to do the heavy lifting. The IAT has been criticized for oversimplifying the complex association between race and bias. However, it can be a useful personal reflection tool.

When I took the test, I had a strong racial bias. Here I am writing a book about equity and social justice, a subject I feel passionately about. How can I have a strong bias against black people? At first, I was mortified but, after reflection, I realized that I am a product of the society and culture in which I live—a society and culture that privileges white people. So what is a counselor to do?

Cultural Proficiency and Ethical Decision Making

If we acknowledge the extent of bias within ourselves as counselors, what is our ethical obligation to our students? The American School Counselor Association (ASCA) position statements and ethical guidelines offer a deep understanding of cultural competency, equity, and social justice for school counselors.

The importance of equity is underscored in the students' rights section in the introduction to the ASCA ethical standards (ASCA, 2016). Student rights are included in the Preamble of the Ethical Standards and serve as a foundation for the ethical responsibility of counselors. The first two rights of students speak specifically to students who have been historically underserved. In the first right, ASCA states that students should be respected and treated with dignity. Beyond that, school counseling programs are charged to be "advocates for and affirm all students from diverse populations" (ASCA, 2016, p. 1). ASCA goes on to call school counselors social justice advocates. If competence levels require additional support, the ethical counselor must consult in order to best serve students. In the second student right, ASCA speaks directly to students who have been historically underserved in educational services. Counselors are charged to take "special care ... to improve overall educational outcomes" for these students (ASCA, 2016, p. 1).

What do student rights look like and sound like in the school building? Consider the following when determining if students that you work with have these rights:

Students should be respected and treated with dignity:

- How do staff members speak to students? Do they treat all students with respect?
- Are some students treated with more respect and dignity than others?
- How do students treat each other?
- Are some students respected and others disregarded?

The school counseling program advocates and affirms all students from diverse populations:

- Do you actively seek to overcome barriers for diverse students?
- Do you disaggregate data by race, socioeconomic status, gender, disabilities, English language learners, and other subgroups to ensure that all students are successful?
- Would your stakeholders identify you as a social justice advocate?

The ethical counselor seeks consultation when they require additional support:

- Do you have questions about the best way to serve some groups of students?
- Do you self-reflect to ensure that you have the skills needed when working with students who are different than you?

Counselors purposefully improve educational services for historically underserved population:

- Do you disaggregate data for historically underserved students to ensure that they have access to all educational services?
- Do you disaggregate higher-level courses (AP, AIG) to determine if any subgroups are underserved?
- Do you advocate for placement practices for advanced coursework and intervention services that ensure the right students are selected?

In the body of the ethical standards, equity and social justice are mentioned 18 times, using strong language that emphasizes that ethical school counselors advocate equity and access for all students and actively remove barriers. Because of our knowledge about implicit biases, it is necessary for counselors to purposefully work for all students and not rely on our attempts to treat all students equally. This is the perception that educators have been working with for many years, yet we see again and again that all students are not being educated equally. Something must change and as school counselors we have an ethical mandate to lead this change.

Beyond ethical standards, ASCA provides position statements with more detailed guidelines for the work of the professional school counselor. We will explore the position statements titled "School Counselor and Equity for all Students" (ASCA, 2012) and "The School Counselor and Cultural Diversity" (ASCA, 2015).

The equity statement focuses on the imperative of school counselors to promote "equitable treatment of all students." This includes: maintaining professional knowledge of students' culture while recognizing that cultures are complex and nuanced, changing over time; informing school staff when changes are occurring within the community of the school; promoting the development of equitable policies and practices; promoting access to rigor for all students; developing plans to address inequitable representation of groups of students in academic programs; working to create an environment where all students feel comfortable seeking support when faced with a problem.

The cultural diversity statement from ASCA (2015, p. 19) has a powerful sentence in its rationale for the statement:

> School counselors develop competences in how prejudice, power, and various forms of oppression … affect self, students and all stakeholders. It is essential that school counselors be more globally responsive and culturally competent in the current educational and social environment.

The work to be globally responsive and culturally competent includes exploring personal beliefs and attitudes, ensuring all students have access to the counseling program, addressing the impact of poverty and class on student achievement, and using data to close the gap between student populations. Cultural competency also includes practicing culturally sensitive counseling, respecting students' rights and ensuring that others do as well, collaborating with stakeholders on school climate, and enhancing the counselor's own cultural competence at the same time as facilitating the cultural awareness of staff members. These are not small tasks and require constant vigilance. As discussed in Chapter 2, the work for equity is much like brushing your teeth, a daily task that is never done.

Moving Forward

You are advancing your cultural competence by reading this work. We began by exploring the history of the achievement gap and the ways that students of color have historically been marginalized in a system that was created to educate white students only. We have investigated white privilege and the way that the privilege of being "unmarked" is perpetuated over and over within our society and culture. We have reflected on the biases that we, as educators and members of our society, likely carry, regardless of our skin color or our explicit beliefs on race and equity. Finally, we have reviewed the ASCA ethical standards and position statements that guide our work with students to highlight the areas that speak to equity and social justice.

As we move forward in this book, you will find activities to guide reflections for yourself, students, and staff. You will hear stories from practicing school counselors about what they are doing to incorporate stakeholders in the work of equity and access for all students. You will hear what has worked and what they would do differently. We will provide scenarios about interrupting racism when you see it, including tips and guidelines to support you. In our systemic change chapter, we share techniques for utilizing data to create systemic change and to enroll support of your administration and leadership team. Lastly, this is not easy work so we explore ideas for handling pushback. Depending on where your school is currently, you may feel that you are taking on the task of equity by yourself. Having a plan to handle criticism will help you to feel empowered to continue your work for students.

As we end the part of this book that provides background knowledge and move toward the actual work, take a moment to review the summary sections of each of the first three chapters to refresh your background knowledge. Your knowledge of the why of inequity will support your ability to find the how of overcoming barriers.

Points to Consider

- Bias can exist whether you consciously agree with it or not.
- We use our explicit, cognitive thought processes to explain away our implicit, automatic responses.
- Ethical standards and position statements from the American School Counselor Association underscore the importance of combating bias and increasing cultural competencies for all school counselors.

References

American School Counselor Association. (2012). *The school counselor and equity for all students.* Alexandria, VA: Author.

American School Counselor Association. (2015). *The school counselor and cultural diversity.* Alexandria, VA: Author.

American School Counselor Association. (2016). *ASCA ethical standards for school counselors.* Alexandria, VA: Author.

Carnoy, M., & Garcia, E. (2017, January 12). *Five key trends in U.S. student performance.* Economic Policy Institute.

Clair, M., & Denis, J. (2015). Racism, sociology of. In *International Encyclopedia of the Social and Behavioral Sciences, 2nd edition.* (Vol. 19, pp. 857–863). New York, NY: Elsevier. Retrieved from http://dx. doi. org/10.1016/B978-0-08-097086-8.32122-5.

Implicit Association Test Corporation. (n.d.). *Preliminary information: Take a demo test.*

Kaiser Family Foundation (2017). *Poverty rate by race/ethnicity* [Interactive data table displaying 2016 poverty data].

National Equity Atlas. (2014). *School poverty, United States.* [Bar charts indicating levels of free-reduced lunch status in the United States].

Nickerson, R. S. (1998). Confirmation bias: A ubiquitous phenomenon in many guises. *Review of General Psychology, 2*, 175–220.

Rury, J. L., & Saatcioglu, A. (2015). Opportunity hoarding. *The Wiley Blackwell Encyclopedia of Race, Ethnicity, and Nationalism.* Hoboken, NJ: John Wiley & Sons. Retrieved from https://doi.org/10.1002/9781118663202.wberen435.

Sim, J. J., Correll, J., & Sadler, M. S. (2013). Understanding police and expert performance: When training attenuates (vs. exacerbates) stereotypic bias in the decision to shoot. *Personality and Social Psychology Bulletin, 39*, 291–304.

U.S. Department of Education, National Center for Education Statistics. *Nation's report card* [Interactive 2013 report outlining average reading scores by race and national school lunch program eligibility].

Part II

Building Change

Chapter 4

The Benefit of Self-Reflection
The Work Begins With You

Interrupting and disrupting racism within a school system as a school counselor happens at different levels. During the school day, we pride ourselves on finding teachable moments with our students. From the time the bell rings until the last student walks out the door, there are a multitude of ways we can impact the lives of our students, our colleagues, our families and ourselves. The following chapter will include multiple levels of systems or ecology, as they relate to interrupting racism within the school environment. When we think of ecology, we think of living and breathing interactions. We think of small to large in size and scope. We might even envision complex maneuvering between these various levels and sizes if we are being comprehensive and thinking globally. As we know, much of what we do outside of school affects us inside of school. Much of where we

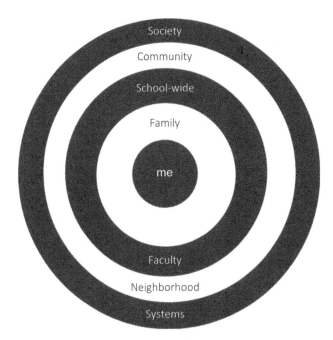

Figure 4.1 The school environment based on Brofenbrenner's Ecological Theory.

Source: Images created by Rebecca Atkins.

come from and how we live will find its way into our professional lives. Our work can vary in scale. We can write a short reflection paragraph about our observation in a classroom or we can plan a school-wide event to counter the negative effects of bullying in our K–12 building. Anticipate some variation in scale. Anticipate much overlap. Anticipate there will be layered and complicated examples to follow in this chapter and in this workbook. The goal is to ensure we are fully developing into the kinds of counselors that can never run out of ways in which we affect change.

Individual

The individual level of ecology allows us to focus on what we are, where we come from and how we develop. When you think of a baby, you think of a human who was born into a family. The family was not chosen. The circumstances were not chosen. Regardless of the born-into situation the child must learn how to function. Let's start there and ask yourself the following questions:

- Who was I born to?
- When was I born?
- What was happening when I was born (in the world, in my state, in my city, in my neighborhood)?
- Describe the situation in which you were born. Was it to a middle-class young white married couple in the suburbs of New Jersey? Do you have no idea because it was a closed adoption and the most anyone can tell you is that a middle-aged, low-income black family from Birmingham decided to make you their daughter?

There are many possible answers. You may even have to do some digging to discover how you came into this world. If you must work diligently for this information, you might ask why that is. These details are relevant because not only do they overlap with familial dynamics which we will explore in a moment, but they also tell part of your story. We learn from those around us just as our students do. During our earliest days, the way in which the people who cared for us perform that care impacts our lives. Chronologically, there is a step-by-step process that occurred in your life. Childhood to adolescence to adulthood, we are socialized in various ways. We become who we are due to the interactions of nature, nurture, society, and all of these things.

Many people's beliefs are shaped by their family while some people's beliefs are the exact opposite of their family's. There are facts about our lives and there are beliefs about or created by our families. Our families tell stories that are windows into shared beliefs, traditions, and perceptions. In this chapter, we will continue to explore how we came to be who we are, how and why our beliefs were shaped as they were, as well as how to undo some of the faulty learning that affects our educating. We might select uncovering the roots to our thinking. Ask yourself:

- Do I share my family's beliefs?
- If so, what is similar? If not, what is different?

- How did I get these beliefs? Was it indirectly? Was it directly?
- Was I told what to believe?
- Why did I, or did I not, go along with that?

We are exploring the inner workings of ourselves so that we might fully embrace the possibility that all of our understanding of ourselves, our beliefs, our values, is flexible and not fixed. There may be inconsistencies and hypocrisies in our belief system. Additionally, we may uncover what so many counselors, educators, and administrators have been buzzing about in recent years: bias. Only then can we appreciate the human ability to transform, grow, and evolve.

Let's dive into this a little deeper. Connect the reasons you became a school counselor to who you are as a person. Think about the chronological steps of your life that led you to the moment you are reading this sentence. Tie your experiences into your beliefs, your values, your personality. You have made many decisions throughout your life and those decisions were influenced by who you are and how you think. For example, my mother enjoyed tutoring as a teenager. She would often help her friends figure out complex problems after school. She enjoyed the feeling of being smarter than other people. The women in our family are educated. She felt a sense of belonging as one of many smart women in our family. She felt she deserved to be seen in this light. She delighted in her teacher's praise. She went to college during the mid-1970s during a time when women in the workplace were becoming more of the norm. The old narrative of a woman staying home in a heteronormative household while the husband went to work was fading quickly. She translated education into economics. She began to believe that the smarter you are the more money you make. As a low-income black girl in North Philly, going to college meant you'd eventually become rich—though this was a product of a faulty belief system in her neighborhood, family, and culture, It influenced her decision to finish college and enter corporate America. She was willing to evolve into a finance-driven person, allowing her need for continued education to take a back seat. She longed for graduate school but was enticed by the money in working. Because she was a person who valued belonging, corporate America quickly became a bore. She traveled throughout the country but was painfully unfulfilled. She spent 60 hours a week in an office with people to whom she barely spoke. The sense of belonging was missing, so she joined a women's group and discovered a colleague was going back to school to become a teacher. The encounter sparked a renewed interest in demonstrating smarts and helping others. One year later, she entered a Masters program for education. She has been a teacher ever since. Now, follow your path and identify the values and beliefs that influenced that path.

Type or handwrite your life map by the year starting as early as you can remember. This may take many pages and many days, weeks, or months, but is a worthwhile reflection. This exercise can seem tedious but may uncover some patterns to your behavior or thoughts that reveal truths you have taken for granted. You may uncover nothing significant at all and that's ok too!

When you have a written life map, we will explore this with a social justice lens. Race is typically not discussed openly in positive ways, though it is as American as apple pie and denim jeans. In order to redefine some of our thinking and

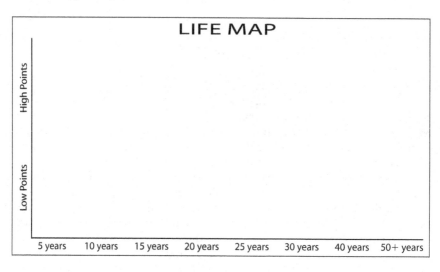

Figure 4.2 Complete your own life map, placing dots along the x and y axis according to
         your experiences. Connect the dots to journey through your life experiences.

Source: Images created by Rebecca Atkins.

behavior, it may be helpful to reflect on how we got to where we are today.
Let's focus on race for a bit:

- How do you define race?
- With which race(s) do you identify?
- How do you know this is your race?
- Are/were your parents/guardians of the same race or different? How did
  they know?
- When did they teach you about race?
- Did you agree with their teachings? Always? Recently? Never?
- In what ways do you express your race?
- Can you separate that out from culture?
- What's the difference? What are the similarities?
- Do you believe that races are different from each other? If so, in what ways?
  If not, how do you justify this, or how did you learn this?
- How have your views about race shifted over time? What influenced those
  shifts?
- In what other ways do you identify? Why are these important to you? How
  are these identifiers expressed in your everyday life?

These questions might also be very helpful to discuss with a trusted peer who is
open to the possibility of exploring race beliefs. Be sure to talk with someone
who will allow you to talk openly and freely without interruption. Stream of
consciousness will often reveal unknowns. Talk without judgement in ways that
are as objective as possible. If your parents taught you that Latino men were kind,
make note of that. If you learned that black girls wear afro puffs and celebrate
Kwanzaa, that will be an important piece to your puzzle as you unpack and
repack your belief system and thus your school counseling practice.

You may be working through this chapter at a snail's pace or simply skimming through. Let's take a pause.

As we work our way through these reflective experiences, it's important to practice self-care. Consider this a reminder to take breaks. Many people will recall upsetting memories or reveal incongruencies in their personal narrative. While working with a former teacher to uncover her biases towards students, the teacher disclosed adolescent trauma in her life. We discussed the possibility that the traumatic experience shaped some of her thinking as a white female educator towards young black males in particular. She wanted to believe that all people were equal and no race was more or less dangerous than another. Her behavior suggested otherwise. She came to realize through reflection that she was, in fact, afraid of her young black male students. Acknowledging this fear was upsetting but a necessary part of her understanding. She had to come to terms with her current behavior and develop new ways of viewing and reacting to black males in her classroom and in her community. Numerous articles and texts have been devoted to self-care. Identify what works for you in a way that allows you to feel safe but doesn't completely extinguish discomfort. To be uncomfortable throughout this book is a necessary part of the process but we also do not want you to suffer and quit. We are tasked to challenge our thoughts in the ways we ask students to give a second and third thought to behaviors or cognitions that might be disrupting their progress. We encourage you to pace yourself but stick with it for long-term growth.

Familial

We must take the time to understand and cope with the people in our lives whom we did not choose. Some of us have families that nurture, encourage, support, and believe in us. Some of us have families who hurt us more than we care to admit. Underlying all of this is a system of values we inherited simply by being born to the people who raised us (or born and then adopted by the people who raised us). Anthony Bowen is a family systems theorist who believes that our upbringing is a complex web of interaction (The Bowen Center, 2018). Our parents operated in their relationship, while the global economy changed for better or worse, while we started our first day of kindergarten in a class of people who probably looked like us, while our father's job industry began to decline, while the world kept turning. If you are reading this book, you were born during a time when America had already formed as a nation, indigenous people have been largely and forcibly isolated on reservations for decades, segregation between whites and people of color was and is still very much present in public schools, computers have become a necessity, and many people believe that success and happiness can be found when one simply works hard. While we exist in our current state, we must take note that the historical context of our current world is relevant and crucial to ensuring we do not make the mistakes of the past.

A family tree is a way for you to better position yourself in the present. Not only is a family tree a way to know your great-grandmother's name and where she came from, but it is a way to provide some circumstance around how we came to be with our own thoughts, beliefs, biases, and experiences. We recognize this is incredibly difficult for some educators who were adopted or no longer have access to elders. Be encouraged to skip this exercise if it is painful. Be diligent about self-care and know that this exploration does not require blood relationships as it is meant to highlight any influential people in your life from birth to present.

To begin, simply find a notebook/journal that is durable, taking account of one's history can be time-consuming. This work is not being done for the sake of knowing, we are actively seeking out how our beliefs may have been shaped and formed. We do not exist in a vacuum. Understanding the hows and whys is therapeutic to some. We are also, through these exercises, able to release some of the burden of our own beliefs in a way that is impersonal and non-threatening. Succinctly, we are learning to not take this personally. Once you have decided on a place to write, start with your life.

- Where were you born and during which time period?
- Do you remember the demographics of your earliest childhood neighborhood?
- Do you remember your siblings' friends?
- How did differences show up in your family, rather, who was different and in what way?
- What did the people in your household do or say about differences, particularly race as it relates to this book.

Explore any details about your childhood experiences for examples to support conclusions and examples to contradict your memories. For instance, when I attended a predominantly white Catholic school I held a belief that all white women had a certain body type. I have no idea how I received that message, but I remember thinking how odd a nun appeared with a voluptuous figure, given that white women were all skinny and tall. This is a unique example but it illustrates how our perceptions are skewed and often incorrect! Spend some time on this. Some of your realizations will be comical like my tall, skinny white woman belief. Some may be more serious and troubling. If you have experienced trauma related to race, it may prove important to recall the circumstances surrounding the incident with a trusted professional. Again, if at any point any of these exercises are too painful, please take care. While exploring race can promote growth, we need to persevere ourselves in a way that will allow us to continue the difficult work.

Next, further detail the dynamic between family members. Across differences, we take for granted the kind of ways in which we interact. We might have had a polite relationship with our uncle in a wheelchair while covertly holding faulty beliefs about ability. Pertaining to race, the movies "Guess Who's Coming To Dinner" and "Get Out" demonstrate ways in which faulty thinking about race creep into our minds and actions (Kramer, 1967; McKittrick, Blum, Hamm, & Peele, 2017). Both movies highlighted the family's culture of politeness. They wanted to seem accepting of differences even though they were not. These themes and patterns are crucial to explore. The common response when confronted with racist thinking or behaviors is to deflect and deny. Additionally, many adults of all races want to prove they are somehow immune to owning prejudices because they belong to a marginalized group. We may see this in our family as relatives who take on incorrect beliefs that because they are not white they cannot be harmful towards people of color. We know this isn't true. We may have relatives who are white and do not believe they can be racist because they are a low-income individual who is nice to their black co-worker. We have all heard the "but I have a black friend" rationale to disassociate from racist thinking. We also know this is not true. Anyone can harbor negative beliefs about another race.

We define racism as a system of power in America that is held by the majority, that operates in ways that disproportionately and negatively affects a race of people. We also know that any person, regardless of race, can be harmful (on individual and small-systems levels—including within families) to marginalized groups. Exploring how this might operate in your family is a necessary part of this self-discovery, especially when these are the people you encounter frequently in your life.

Association with communities of color and belonging to communities of color does not alleviate one of a mindset that devalues people of color. Watch the movies "Guess Who's Coming For Dinner" and "Get Out" and continue to write about your own family. Discuss with living relatives their perceptions of difference and their interaction across difference. What did grandmother think of having a son in a wheelchair? How did aunt Susan respond to cousin Sarah's new Asian boyfriend? Did she talk to my mom about it in secret? What did dad say after the planes crashed into the twin towers on September 11th? Why does aunt Carol still call white people "Caucasians"? Don't stop writing until you uncover some truths!

Student-Educator/Counselor Dynamic

Just about every counselor and educator is asked to create a philosophy of practice at some point in their career. We are tasked to reveal how we believe we might impact our students. Most of us want to be helpers, listeners, and encouragers. Rarely do counselors consider themselves to be agents of change in a racist society. According to Dr. Erin Mason, a counselor educator at Georgia State University:

> When we train school counselors, we have a responsibility to prepare them to be competent with an ever-diversifying population of students. In order for them to be agents of change at multiple levels, dedicated discussion of historic and current forces of racism, oppression, and marginalization must be part of graduate training. Ignoring these issues does a disservice to their future P-12 students and families, and minimizing them keeps the profession from being able to recruit and retain a diverse workforce.

A counselor educator from the California State University at Long Beach agrees. Dr. Caroline Lopez-Perry states:

> Our educational system is systematically racist in a number of ways including unequal funding in schools, the school-to-prison pipeline that disproportionally affects students of color, and racial bias in standardized testing. School counselors must be trained on how to identify and eliminate oppressive

structures within students' educational setting and the surrounding community. As civil rights activist Bayard Rustin once said, "We need, in every community, a group of angelic troublemakers." As such, graduate programs should prepare school counselors to develop, as agents of change, the skills necessary to dismantle oppressive systems. This includes deliberately developing and practicing: 1) the habits and abilities of forming and reforming collaborative relationships with colleagues, parents, and community members, 2) career-long learning and personal reflection on improvement of practice, and 3) having a voice at the policy level.

Within our graduate programs, we may have registered and taken courses on multiculturalism. In a review of the Council for Accreditation of Counseling and Related Educational Programs, most school counselor training contains at least two mandatory courses related to understanding the implications of identity, race, and class in the classroom. Cultural diversity must be implemented within the degree or certification curriculum. The textbook *Culturally Proficient Collaboration* notes that "school counselors serve as leaders who advocate for the needs and services of all students in K-12, and identify systemic inequities that hinder access to resources for students who are underserved" (Stephens & Lindsey, 2011, p. 58). In order to identify barriers, resource-gaps, and needs, counselors must be equipped to learn *from* and learn *for* their students. We must be willing and able, open and ready to receive our students experiences. We must be prepared to believe our students tell us about their emotional and psychological processes as they develop into young adults. Let's explore balancing the two worlds of learning from and learning for our students.

A culturally sensitive, attuned, and aware counselor does not place the responsibility to educate the educator on people of color. In other words, it's not fair to require a student to teach you how to be culturally aware. The role of the student is participating and receiving education. The role of the educator, including teachers, counselors, and administrators, is to facilitate education. By altering the dynamic by which students and educator operate within a school system, tangential shifts occur that place students in harm's way. For example, an elementary school counselor who leans on a Ghanaian student to teach the class about being raised in Ghana is using his/her authority as the counselor to give the student the role of educator. Not only is this unfair to the Ghanaian student who may or may not be aware of the diversity that exists within the country of Ghana, but it releases any responsibility other students have in exploring the world around them. Having one student speak for a group can be demoralizing and inaccurate. We then need to balance this risk with students being in a position to share their cultural perspective in a way that may teach others. There can be space for students to educate other students and the counselor. However, this must be done in a way that is humanizing, equalizing, and voluntary.

Central High School in Philadelphia is a shining example of how multiculturalism is encouraged and celebrated in ways that are inclusive and voluntary. Students have autonomy when deciding to share or not share their cultural or racial experience. It is not assigned to them, particularly not without warning. Central hosts a school-wide "International Day" where students take the lead planning and preparing for the day-long event. Some students agree to create and serve food that represents their families, some create a show for all students with dancing and music. Students spend the entire day dressed in fashion that demonstrates their family's home country. The event is not an administrator, teacher, or counselor assignment or directive. When the students can take ownership of their culture or race, including teaching others, the outcome is less harmful to that student. This idea extends into college, when black students are often the only black student in a predominantly white college course. Each student in that college course should be accustomed to exploring issues of difference on their own so as to not make the one student in class the representative for all. Time and time again, we hear these experiences from students at PWIs (predominantly white institutions) and even in the workforce. Now is the time to help all children and all adults learn when to encourage volunteering information without pressure, without directives or expectations. Now is the time to end the reliance on people of color to be the teachers in this instance.

Tim Wise is an author, activist, and historian who tells about the time he encounters a person of color on a humanistic level. "I remember the first time I ever saw a black person … I mean *really* saw them … white folks have always felt the right to define black and brown folks' realities for them" (2008, p. 29). He tells about a time when, as a young child looking out of his home window, he was introduced to the concept of race. He learned through reading and the gentle guidance of his mother, who did not typically shy away from discussions of race, that black and white people are treated differently in America. While in college, Wise acquired the training and information necessary to responsibly be an ally to people of color. From this work, he witnessed first-hand differing experiences of white people and black people. The differences were pervasive. He decided to speak up about it. It's crucial that as counselors we believe the emotional and psychological experiences of our students, particularly our marginalized students. Too often, marginalized communities of color are unquestionably associated with negativity. Poor black girls are thought of as mean and unapproachable. Outgoing Latino boys are regarded as gang-affiliated and unable/unwilling to speak English (even though there is nothing wrong with preferring Spanish). The benefit of the doubt is lost with children of color. At this end of the pendulum, the feelings and thoughts of young people of color are not nearly as important as controlling these students in the classroom guised as intensive, unrelenting, and uncompassionate classroom management.

When the need for student support is recognized, the opposite end of the pendulum is problematic. The "White Savior" is an idea that children of color need to be saved from themselves, their families, and their surroundings, but counselors of any race can take on this identity. Chris Emdin, author of *White Folks Who Teach in the Hood, and All the Rest of Y'all Too*, suggests

> providing … teachers [with] … tools to allow them to be able to develop pedagogical strategies that they need. This work is, in many ways, a labor of love … there are more white teachers in urban spaces than ever before, and oftentimes they come from backgrounds that don't reflect the backgrounds of students, so those folks need as much help as possible. But the book is also named for "the rest of y'all too." This is for black teachers who oftentimes take on the structures of traditional schooling and are just as ineffective. The

work is about providing tools to make you better at your craft and do right by young people.

(Education Week, 2016, audio interview)

Several activities can help illustrate these points. The first is a familiar technique called the audit. There are many types of audits but we will tailor this to our counselor-student relationship.

- First, write your counseling philosophy.
- What does it say?
- What does it include? What does it exclude?
- Find examples throughout the past week that honor all the parts of your philosophy and think of the students who were involved.
    - Did they share commonalities? Were they all high-achieving?
    - Were they all able-bodied? Were they all white?
    - Were they all "well-behaved"?
- Notice any patterns and make a list.
- Rewrite your philosophy until it becomes more inclusive.

Counselors love surveys! Survey your students to find out if they know you. What do they think of you? Children are wonderfully honest and perceptive. They might likely tell you what you are doing wrong or to which types of students you seem to cater. Ask your students if they know who you are supposed to help the most. If they say "sad" students or students who "are being bad" then this may be a window into how your practice is or isn't equitable. Counselors often have to be all things to everyone, but we can find a balance and a rhythm that not only works for us, but also serves the students in beneficial and efficient ways. Intention isn't the goal. We must put into practice the philosophies that best serve our populations. Just because a philosophy is practiced does not mean it is best practice for your kids.

Counselor-Teacher/Administration

The language shifts each year. Recently, we have enforced the term "people of color" and by the time this book is on every shelf of every school, there will be new terms. We have to accept that change is inevitable. What was once acceptable will someday be outdated and possibly even offensive. We no longer refer to black people as "Negroes" or "colored people." How then do we expect to learn what is new? Who is supposed to teach what we need to know? How can we hold each other accountable and continue to work collaboratively?

During the American School Counselors Association Conference of 2016 in New Orleans, a young white woman approached me about working with her black colleagues. She seemed frustrated. I asked her to elaborate on her concern. She told me that as a white woman at her school, she feels "wrong" correcting black women on the effects of racism at her school. She told me that she understands how racism negatively impacts the school community but some black teachers and administrators do not believe racism is a factor. I was inspired in many ways to respond to her concern. As a black woman, I am often empowered to speak up about racist beliefs and behaviors whether those beliefs are held by white or black people. As a member of the marginalized group, I am in a position to speak on my experience and the experiences of others who look like me. Now, here I am standing in this conference hall surrounded by all shades of white, tan, and brown. I wasn't stumped. I knew I wanted to encourage this young white woman to call out any instance of inequity. I knew that this response was just a part of the action that needed to take place at her school if these attitudes were affecting student outcomes. "Call-out culture" has been a growing and oftentimes controversial topic as individuals are becoming more frustrated with covert racism in all of the ways it's presented in everyday life. Call-out happens when someone says or does something negatively impactful on a marginalized community and as a response someone acknowledges the behavior and states that it is unacceptable. In this person's school, black female administrators made a joke about the number of special education students at a school. In the joke, they attributed the special needs to derogatory terms for mothers on public assistance. The white woman told the administrators that they were inappropriate. She also told them that their attitude towards the families of special education children was harmful to students. In cultures that are not "call-out," the white educator who approached me at the conference would not have voiced her objection.

Immediately after call-out culture as a whole began receiving critiques, the concept of white fragility became more popular as a response. What we have now is a communication dynamic that revolves around oppressed groups, speaking out about oppression and all related emotions. These are ideas that we must be prepared to understand as we enter into deep reflection, courageous conversations, and social justice actions. Call-out culture can be managed with veracity and empathy. Professional development (PD) is another way to address how we choose to collaborate with colleagues. PD allows us to increase our social justice tools and gives us a safe space in which we can practice the language of courageous conversations. There is often quite a lot of practice involved in this work because, again, we are not socialized to discuss race. Educators, especially counselors, are tasked with diving into the trenches of race-related conversation and action.

In the history of public education, we learned how racism and discrimination impacted the hiring practices of black and white teachers throughout the country. We know the impact of such practices linger into the twenty-first century. Many schools are working to view their faculty with a race lens as the number of students of color increases throughout the country. A simple demographics assessment has likely already been conducted at your school.

- What are the racial demographics of your school's leadership?
- What are the demographics of your school's student body?
- What are the demographics of your teachers and educators?
- What do these percentages reflect/mean?
- What are the demographics of the neighborhood surrounding your school?

Share this information at your next faculty meeting, Professional Learning Community, or counseling team meeting and ask your colleagues if these numbers reflect anything to them. Log responses to later detect any patterns in the beliefs of your staff. As you reflect on your practice, you are more likely to be in tune with what may be problematic about your school or what works well. As we lean into this discovery with our race lens, we can anticipate further action for the future. Based on the feedback of educators to the comparative analysis of racial demographics, counselors can identify where further professional development is necessary. For example, say a few teachers believe the school is all black because of the neighborhood. We have learned throughout this book and possibly other learnings that housing segregation is ongoing and naturally affects where students attend school. We have also learned that busing programs allow black children to attend predominantly white schools. We can self-reflect with the following questions:

- Why is our school predominantly black or white or racially integrated?
- Is our surrounding community segregated? Why might that be?
- How might our school benefit from having more racially diverse classes or is it best we remain all black or white?

Another example might be, a teacher suggests students' low achievement is due to lack of family engagement. We see this belief quite often. What we have learned from this book and other sources, however, teaches us that black and brown communities have endured centuries of negative associations with the system of education. The trust that is assumed to be earned by schools can often be nonexistent in some communities.

- How might I call-out this stereotype in a way that invites the teacher into dialogue?
- What information is most helpful for the teacher to understand about achievement in black students?
- How can I stress the importance of the work of building trust across race?
- In what ways can we take more ownership of cultivating relationships as leaders in the community?
- Does parental engagement lead to better education outcomes for all children? Do we have data on this? Additionally, how much parental involvement is best for my developmental group of students?
- How can I be careful of attributing lack of engagement to a self-deprecating desire to remain uneducated?
- How might I help faculty understand that parents want their children to be educated? Often, parents, particularly those of low income, suffer the hardships of poverty that do not afford them the flexibility, energy, or time to engage in a system that has historically been exclusive.
- As the school counselor, how have I called out these faulty beliefs in the past? What has worked and what has not?

Self-reflection activities may be especially helpful when the relationship experiences at school have proven to be contentious. Tension may have many sources. Tension can also linger and affect our relationships with colleagues. Let's be honest, faculty members fall and blunder just as we do. We must remember that we are all on a journey of progress. Engaging in this work requires compassion for yourself, your family, and your co-workers. Many people want to get better at the work of educating children. Every person has experiences related to their family and life and brings those experiences to the conversation. Gentleness with yourself and others can foster a sense of hope during the most difficult of times.

- How am I being gentle with myself during these explorations of self-reflection?
- How forgiving am I?
- How have I been forgiven in the past? What happened?
- What are some thoughts I have about my colleagues? About my administrators?
- How do these thoughts influence my interactions with them?

School-Wide

We are the creators of safe spaces. In more recent history, safe spaces are highly politicized. People identify with the right or the left or somewhere in between. These polarized systems of thought have forced the conversation to be more about the holder of the belief than the person affected by the belief. In schools, we have long held the standard that as counselors, we are not only a safe person to confide in but we are also a person who will provide a safe building, community, and overall learning environment. Regardless of one's political affiliation, education is a field where the child's wellbeing is of utmost importance. The safe building, community, and learning environment are all within our ability to influence.

Healthy environments produce the kinds of students who want to be in school, who trust faculty and administrators, and who are engaged with the learning process. Engagement in school leads to better outcomes regardless of socioeconomic class, race, and various other factors. Imagine a school with high engagement. What does that look like to you? Faculty and administrators can be seen interacting positively with students. Counselors greet students as they enter the building with a smile and a high five. These are the types of connections children crave and remember, even when they are having difficulty. School counselors are often the keepers of school culture. We are tasked to survey, develop, and implement the strategies necessary for our school to be a place of learning, wellbeing, and growth. We collaborate with teachers, administrators, community-based organizations and families to create programs that benefit all students, leaving no child excluded. We are the creators and we need to continue to create in ways that will naturally, as a result, benefit the world.

Assessing school culture can be done in similar ways as assessing student-counselor relationships. Receiving feedback from students can be tricky. On any given day, an eight-year old with a grudge to bear can complain about how much he hates school, especially if he served detention the night before. Teenagers are particularly fickle with their opinions, feeling strongly about one person at the beginning of the week and feeling entirely different by the end. Overall, like any sample size, as many students should be polled as possible. Individual anecdotes might also be useful when you are aware of the context in which it was given. Counselors also need to be sure their assessments are reliable and valid. Examples of tried and true assessments include *The School Leader's Tool for Assessing School Culture*, included in Appendix 3, created by Christopher Wagner (2006). In this assessment, school leadership is able to determine the climate in which they operate. The details of these results will shine light on how well the school is supported to begin or continue difficult race work.

Additionally, the School Culture Survey by the Georgia Leadership Institute for School Improvement (GLISI) offers counselors a glimpse into how positive the culture is when beginning or continuing this work (GLISI, 2016). Using multiple assessments allows for increased reliability.

As it pertains to race, we must turn on and/or adjust our lens. We can adapt these questions or interpret their answers, accounting for specific groups, to ascertain whether or not our race culture at school is healthy, thriving, and promoting development for every child within our school. The Colorado Department of Education created an Equity Toolkit that can be adapted by school districts across the nation (2010). What the toolkit tries to evaluate is the manner in which the students, faculty, and administrators treat race-related issues. Their resource is a great abbreviated complement to this workbook.

- Which assessments have been chosen for the school to assess climate?
- How will the students be involved in the assessments? Will parents be involved? Any other stakeholders?
- What information do we hope to capture?
- What hypotheses can be made before receiving results? What evidence for these hypotheses exists?
- After assessments are completed, were there any conflicting messages or data points?
- Were there any surprises?
- What are the next steps to resolve what might be problematic about the school's culture? Who needs to be involved with next steps?

Intersectional Identity

Intersectional identity, as it relates to race, is the overlapping and intertwined nature of people. The intersection of race and sibling order or gender and affluence are examples of how complex the human condition is. We have described identity above and you have connected your experiences with how you express yourself as a person. Let us reflect on the following questions:

- What are two of your identifiers that intersect congruently? How do two identifiers have similar experiences?

  If you are a black woman, you may identify being black and being a woman as two characteristics that share similar experiences of scrutiny or unreasonable expectations. If you are a person who identifies as LGBTQ and come from a poor working-class family, you may view these characteristics as having similar experiences of judgement or shame or even, conversely, self-drive and pride.

- What are two of your identifiers that intersect incongruently?

  For example, being born into a wealthy family and Spanish-speaking or being young in age and burnt out from stressful work.

Unravel the complexities of intersectional identity in your life. By doing this, you can identify even deeper, more complex ways your belief system has been shaped.

Self-reflection involves multi-level insight. Self-reflection is designed to increase awareness and understanding. Each level of insight offers a layer of information that can help inform school counselor's practice. All of the levels offer counselors an opportunity to detail, examine, and question their life experiences in a way that shapes their understanding of social justice perspectives. This chapter has offered many questions to the many layers of our lives. With gentle pursuit, the goal is to gain clarity. Having clarity about one's past can lead to informed and positive possibilities for the future. A lack of clarity can stifle one's ability to change and grow.

Points to Consider

- There are multiple levels of self-reflection that can unveil patterns of thoughts, beliefs, biases, and behaviors.
- Exploring family systems can uncover the earliest experiences of race.
- Maintaining counselor–educator relationships can prove difficult when interrupting racism. Self-care and discernment is an important part of that process.
- The complexities of identity overlap, leading to many different ways in which we can experience our privileges and oppressions. Intersectional identity can help us sort through and unpack these characteristics.
- Examining the past can help create opportunities for growth in the future.

References

Bowen Center. (2018). *About—The Bowen Center*. Retrieved from https://thebowencenter.org/about.

Bronfenbrenner Center for Translational Research. (2014). *About us: Bronfenbrenner Center for Translational Research*. Retrieved from www.bctr.cornell.edu/about-us.

Colorado Department of Education. (2010). *Equity toolkit for administrators*. Retrieved from www.cde.state.co.us/postsecondary/equitytoolkit.

Education Week (Distributor). (2016, August 30). Q&A with Christopher Emdin: Reaching Students of Color. [Audio interview]. In *Education Week Commentary*.

Georgia Leadership Institute for School Improvement. (2016). *School Culture Survey*. Retrieved from http://glisi.org/wp-content/uploads/2015/08/School-Culture-Survey_GLISI.pdf.

Kramer, S. (Producer and Director). (1967). "Guess who's coming to dinner." [Motion picture]. United States: Columbia Pictures.

McKittrick, S., Blum, J., Hamm, E. H. (Prods.), & Peele, J. (Director). (2017). *Get out*. [Motion picture]. United States: Universal Pictures.

Stephens, D. L., & Lindsey, R. B. (2011). *Culturally proficient collaboration: Use and misuse of school counselors*. Thousand Oaks, CA: Corwin SAGE.

Wagner, C. (2006). The school leader's tool for assessing and improving school culture. *Principal Leadership, 7*(4), 41–44.

Wise, T. (2008). *White like me: Reflections on race from a privileged son*. Berkeley, CA: Soft Skull Press.

Chapter 5

Teach Them Well
Anti-Bias Social Emotional Learning for Students

When students enter the school building on the first day of kindergarten, we start at the beginning. We make no assumptions that they know anything about reading, math, or even how to behave in school. Kindergarten teachers are masters at starting from scratch to build the capacity of all students in the room to work and learn as a classroom community. As students get older, our expectations of what they already know and have mastered rise. We know what has been taught in the previous year and so we know where to continue building knowledge. Expanding beyond academics and into the realm of social emotional learning is encouraging and exciting. Positive behavioral interventions and support (PBIS) and multi-tiered system of support (MTSS) have brought behavior into the realm of core instruction in ways that we have not previously seen.

There's one thing we're not talking about—race and equity. As a society, we treat race as a taboo subject. It's not "polite conversation" or we insist that we are "color blind." We've discussed in previous chapters why these concepts don't serve you as a counselor or your staff as educators. However, we have not explored the importance of discussing race with students.

Students can't be expected to know something they were never taught. Dr. Brigitte Vittrup, a child development expert, states:

> It sends a very loud message to the children that this topic is taboo. While the intended message may be "Shhh.... Race is a sensitive topic in this country, so be careful what you say out loud, because we don't want to offend anybody," what the child is more likely to hear is "Shhh ... there's something wrong with these people, so let's not talk about them."
>
> (Vittrup, 2015)

If we treat race and equity as taboo subjects at school, students will quickly learn that race is a forbidden topic and come to their own conclusions based on what they observe in their immediate surroundings.

We might not like the conclusions students make because the world they live in is full of racism, bias, and privilege. If students walk by the AIG room and see mostly white students, will they conclude that white students are smarter than black students? If students walk by the basketball team and see mostly black students, will they conclude that all black people are good at sports? We must explicitly teach our students what racism is, why it's unfair, and how to confront it.

For our K-8 students, we have created lesson plans for direct instruction during social emotional learning. High-school lesson plans can be implemented in class, during advisory, seminar, after-school workshop events, and within clubs. These lesson plans use the Teaching Tolerance Social Justice standards, available in Appendix B. In the Teaching Tolerance standards, there are four domains of anti-bias education: Identity, Diversity, Justice, and Action. The Identity and Diversity domains aim to reduce prejudice and the Justice and Action domains aim to move students toward collective action. The Standards include 20 anchor standards, five within each domain or goal. In addition, each standard has a corresponding grade level outcome for K-2, 3–5, 6–8, and 9–12.

Identity

The goal of the Identity domain is that "each child will demonstrate self-awareness, confidence, family pride, and positive social identities" (Teaching Tolerance, 2017). In younger grades, we look to help children increase self-confidence and understand their own strengths and the positive attributes of their cultural identities. For instance, a child whose mother wears a hijab would be able to demonstrate that they understand the cultural significance of the hijab and communicate pride in their social identity as a Muslim. As children grow older, they will begin to question their social identities and we look to help older children to reflect on their multiple identities and to celebrate both their in-group and out-group identities, we anticipate the approach to complex thoughts about race and identity. For instance, a teenager who is biracial may experience conflicting treatment from both sides of their family. A struggle to "choose sides" might ensue.

Diversity

The goal of the Diversity domain is that "each child will express comfort and joy with human diversity accurate language for human differences; and deep, caring human connections" (Teaching Tolerance, 2017). For younger students, they will learn that families and individuals are different and that these differences add value to the community we live in. For instance, younger students may learn about different traditions within their own community or around the world. In older students, we want to add an emphasis on the importance of actively learning about people, cultures, and communities different than your own. We want to be able to exchange ideas and beliefs in a respectful way. This might look like conversations in the classroom about controversial current events with an emphasis on the process of high-intensity discussions.

Justice

The goal of the Justice domain is that "each child will increasingly recognize unfairness, have language to describe unfairness, and understand that unfairness hurts" (Teaching Tolerance, 2017). It might seem that younger students understand fairness with the regularity that you hear "that's not fair" in an elementary school. However, younger students may need considerable support in understanding unfairness in relation to interpersonal skills and conflicts. Younger students also have less real-world experience and should be exposed to stories of unfairness and injustice with examples of people who worked to stop the injustice. As students grow older, they can expand this knowledge to examples of injustice that are outside of their own experiences. They can also build on their understanding of the nuances of the work of ending injustice. For example, labor rights have improved in some areas but not in others, or for undocumented immigrants.

Action

The goal of the Action domain is that "each child will demonstrate empowerment and the skills to act, with others or alone, against prejudice and discriminatory actions" (Teaching Tolerance, 2017). One of the joys of working with children is their pure excitement and motivation to act. If we are to build their understanding of their identity, the benefits of diversity, and the just and unjust world, we also want to empower them to act. In younger grades, their actions will likely happen within their classroom or school building. Perhaps they will build a buddy bench on the playground for kids who don't have someone to play with or they will promote a food drive for food-insecure families within the school or community. In older students, the action truly has no limit. An example of action by high-school students is the March for our Lives Movement started by Parkland High School students to end gun-violence in schools.

In the previous year, I have worked with a school counselor in my district, Lauren Brand, to create lesson plans for grade K-5. Incidents had been reported of students being teased or excluded because of their religion, race, or special needs. As a result of this, Lauren and I decided that we would create a scope and sequence of developmental competencies for equity as a global concept. We moved students through the idea that differences are valuable, inclusion is important, and that equity supports relationships with people. After sharing our anti-bias lessons with other counselors within our district, a group of middle-school counselors approached me about creating something similar for students in grades 6–8. Working with this team, we developed lessons with the themes of Who Am I, Who Are You, and What Can We Do.

Elementary

Kindergarten through first grade students are developmentally in the preoperational stage and are imaginative thinkers, but still struggle with abstract concepts. They are egocentric and think first of themselves. School counselors can build on this egocentrism by relating to the child's own schema revolving around differences. In our lessons, we explored the child's traits using self-portraits, traditions, and other activities focusing on the child's schema of self-value. Once we connected their value for self, we were able to connect the idea to value for others.

You can see that we built upon the ideas and worked from self, to others, and then to cooperation or working together. We began to prepare students for the exploration of empathy in second and third grade by relating the positive feelings of cooperation and acceptance to the negative feelings of the opposite. Most K-1 students can understand the feelings of others well, but some cannot. Counselors can expect some scaffolding and support for students who struggle with this idea.

It was also important that we related the lessons to the ASCA Mindsets and Behaviors. In K-1, we focused on the Mindset "Sense of belonging in the school environment," and then the social skills of creating positive and supportive relationships with other students, using effective oral and written communication skills and listening skills, and to demonstrate collaboration and cooperation skills. All of these skills are highly valued by stakeholders and can increase the buy-in for including equity lessons in your curriculum plan at the K-5 level.

Kindergarten Lessons

Title	Learning Objectives	Activity
Be*YOU*tiful You	ID.K-2.1* I know and like who I am and can talk about my family and myself and name some of my group identities. DI.K-2.6 I like being around people who are like me and different from me, and I can be friendly to everyone.	Recognizing similarities and differences within our classroom.
Different is Beautiful	DI.K-2.8 I want to know about other people and how our lives and experiences are the same and different. DI.K-2.9 I know everyone has feelings, and I want to get along with people who are similar and different from me.	Discuss differences and the strengths that each difference has. Have children find differences with BINGO with their classmates.
I Am Special	JU.K-2.12 I know when people are treated unfairly. AC.K-2.20 I will join with classmates to make our classroom fair for everyone.	Read a book (see the Celebrating Diversity Book List in Appendix A) that introduces differences between students. Students can create a Venn diagram showing how they are similar and different.

Note
* See Appendix B for Teaching Tolerance Social Justice Standards.

Be*YOU*tiful You

The class begins by reading a book about differences. Students can discuss the differences that they observe in the classroom. Often, our Kindergarteners are concrete thinkers and often concentrate their focus on physical differences. We honor these physical differences (like skin color) but we also want to help students to see the similarities and differences beyond physical descriptions. To help, use a clipart drawing of butterflies and ask students to fill in the sections of the butterfly answering questions about themselves. For instance, color the dots on the wings the color of your favorite food. Once students have reflected on their own traits, they can compare and contrast with other students in their class. As we've learned, we can't expect students to infer the lesson we are trying to teach about race and equity. Make connections between students by observing, "You have sandy tan skin and you have tawny skin. You both say yellow is your favorite color." Use the actual names of crayons to describe skin colors and make observations that show similarities and differences without judgement value.

Different is Beautiful

Just like adults, kids like things that are familiar. It makes sense, we feel connected to people, places, habits, and appearances that we find in ourselves. It's important that we explicitly teach that differences are good and make our world a better place. In this lesson, I created a slideshow of pictures I found online that show differences.

HIGHLIGHTED DIFFERENCES:

- Children running and playing with children in wheelchairs
- Hands with an array of skin colors
- An older woman holding a young child
- A woman speaking with a sign language interpreter
- Children working in class, one child wearing a hijab
- Children lined up with different heights

After discussing the similarities and differences, I asked students what differences we have that we can't see. Answers can range from personality traits to learning differences. Finally, I made a friendship bingo with picture cues and asked students to find classmates that filled each of the attributes listed.

FRIENDSHIP BINGO:

- Isn't afraid of spiders
- Likes vanilla more than chocolate
- Recycles
- Has a superhero name
- Is happy today
- Can ride a bike
- Has brown eyes
- Can name a dinosaur
- Likes pizza

I Am Special

In the third lesson for Kindergarten, I often read the book *Star Bellied Sneetches* by Dr. Seuss. In this book, the sneetches who have stars are superior to those that do not. The "Fix-It-Up Chappie" comes along with a machine that can put stars on any sneetch. Of course, once everyone has stars on "thars," some sneetches want their stars removed. This goes on and on with sneetches getting stars and not getting stars. Students love this book! After reading, I ask students what kinds of things we, as humans, think are important and make us better than others? Most of the time, Kindergarten students will answer with material possessions like clothes or toys. Sometimes, a student might answer with an attribute like being good at sports. Over the years that I have taught this lesson, occasionally I will have students answer with "the color of our skin." I love it when this happens! We have a wonderful discussion about skin colors and tones. The look on a five-year old's face when you explain that some people think that skin color makes them more important is priceless.

So why didn't I introduce this concept for the kids? I was nervous. What if I was accused of being racist or bringing up topics too complex for the students? I know better now. I know that children see and understand color. I know that students may infer from our taboo treatment of race that race is important but not to be spoken of. I know that if we don't confront inequities due to race, they will continue.

First Grade Lessons

Title	Learning Objectives	Activity
Self Portraits	ID.K-2.4 I can feel good about myself without being mean or making other people feel bad. JU.K-2.11 I know my friends have many identities but they are always still just themselves.	Show exemplars of self-portraits from a diverse range of people. Have students brainstorm what they want people to know about them and how you would express this in a self portrait. Students will draw a self portrait.
Traditions	ID.K-2.2.5 I see that the way my family and I do things is both the same as and different from how other people do things, and I am interested in both. DI.K-2.10 I find it interesting that groups of people believe different things and live their lives in different ways.	Study differences and similarities through traditions. Book: *The Jelly Donut Difference* by Maria Dismondy. Students will create a classroom quilt of their own family traditions.
Cooperate with Differences	JU.K-2.13 I know that life is easier for some people and harder for others and the reasons for that are not always fair. AC.K-2.17 I will say something or tell an adult if someone is being hurtful, and will do my part to be kind even if I don't like something they say or do.	Tower of Cooperation—students each have one "skill" they can use to help their team build a tower of paper and tape. Read "Danika's Differences" in this chapter. Connect the skills they brought to the tower creation to skills they have in real life.

Self-Portraits

We each have things about ourselves that we are proud of, that we like, or that we want the world to see. In this lesson, I showed a series of self-portraits from a diverse group of artists. One of the most recognizable, Frida Kahlo, showcases an attribute that distinguishes her but would be considered undesirable by most people—the unibrow. This is an excellent conversation starter about how the world sees us versus how we see ourselves. I lead a discussion with students asking them, "What do you want others to know about you?" I encourage them to think about what's on the inside. After we brainstorm attributes that students want to highlight, we create self portraits that highlight these attributes. For instance, a student who says they are caring might draw hearts for eyes. A student who says that they are strong might draw big muscles.

Traditions

Schools often include traditions in lessons and learning. Does your school include a variety of traditions outside the normal Christmas, Hanukkah, and Kwanzaa? There are so many more traditions that we can add to our conversation! In this lesson, I show students a variety of pictures that highlight traditions around the world.

TRADITIONS HIGHLIGHTED:

- Traditional coffee service in Colombia
- The backyard cookout
- Chinese New Year
- Yom Kippur
- Christmas
- Henna designs

Students think-pair-share about a tradition that their family celebrates or that they want their family to celebrate. I make sure to incorporate the idea of new traditions because not all students may have a positive home life with heart-warming traditions to share. Students then decorate a paper square with their tradition and we glue on poster board to create a tradition quilt. Some students may not know what a quilt is, this can be a new tradition they learn about!

Cooperate with Differences

Have you ever had to work with someone who had a completely different work style than you? It's hard! Even as adults, we are still mastering the skill of cooperating with differences. Remembering that students at this age are still very concrete thinkers, I created a task for them to complete with differences assigned to them. In groups of four, they were to create a tower using paper and tape. Each student had an assigned role.

ASSIGNED ROLES:

- Paper Specialist—the only person that can touch the paper
- Tape Specialist—the only person that can touch the tape
- Fixer—the only person that can fix and adjust the tower
- Captain—the only person that can give others directions

The group then worked together to create the tallest tower they could. As the counselor, it was important for me to walk around and support their cooperation and help students to work together. The learning in this activity comes from the doing, so expect difficulties and bumps along the way. After the activity, make sure to take time to talk about what worked, what didn't, what was hard, and how to overcome it. Finally, to relate our concrete learning to real life, I read the story of Danika's Differences.

Danika's Differences

By Rebecca Atkins

Hey! My name is Danika. I like to run, read, and ride my bike as much as possible. I guess I'm like most kids except that I have learning differences.

That means it takes me a bit longer than my classmates to learn new things. Most of the time, I don't mind working really hard but sometimes it makes me frustrated or sad.

One day in class, we were working on writing about our family traditions. I was so excited to share how my family's tradition is to each have a half a cupcake on our half birthday. We even put a candle in it! It's really fun.

Anyway, while I was working, I heard a girl in my class say...

What's your family tradition? Being Stupid?

I couldn't believe she would say something so mean! I thought we were friends. I thought about it all day until I got on the bus.

When I got home, I asked my mom what she thought I should do and she said...

Brainstorm with the class:

- *Is it OK to treat others badly because they are different?*
- *Do you think Danika is not smart because she has learning differences?*
- *What kinds of things can you imagine that Danika is really great at?*
- *What advice would you give Danika?*

My mom gave me some great advice and the next day I went to talk to my friend to tell her that what she said hurt my feelings. I mean, I know I have learning differences, but that was just wrong. She apologized and I accepted.

I said "You know what I am really good at? Soccer! Want me to show you how to dribble the ball?" We had a blast at recess that day!

Second and third grade students are moving into the concrete operational stage of cognitive development. In this stage, children are able to think logically about concrete events and grasping concrete analogies. They benefit from learning that presents a progression of ideas from step to step. They are also able to classify and group objects at increasingly complex levels. At this age, they are also shifting their focus from a family orientation to a peer orientation. With an increased focus on peers and better ability to classify and group at complex levels, it makes sense that children will begin to classify those around them.

In our second and third grade lessons we focus on the ASCA Mindsets and Behaviors of demonstrating empathy and the ability to assume responsibility, effective coping skills when faced with a problem, gathering evidence and considering multiple perspectives to make informed decisions, and demonstrating leadership and teamwork skills to work effectively in diverse teams.

Students at this age are still developing their understanding that others experience the world in different ways. They are able to experience and express empathy when they can personally relate to a situation. For instance, if a classmate falls and is hurt, a child has experienced physical pain and can express deep empathy for the pain of their classmate. Have you ever spoken to a child who was mean to another and asked them, "How would you feel if this happened to you?" only to have them reply that it wouldn't bother them. It may be that, in this case, the offender really wouldn't have been bothered by similar teasing or that they have never been so teased and thus cannot understand that the other child's experience or response may differ from theirs.

Second Grade Lessons

Title	Learning Objectives	Activity
The Empathy Puzzle	DI.K-2.9 I know everyone has feelings, and I want to get along with people who are similar to and different from me.	Puzzle of the Heart Game—practice the five skills of empathy:
		* Look and Listen * Remember * Imagine * Ask * Care.
	AC.K-2.16 I care about those who are treated unfairly.	
Someone Else's Shoes	ID.K-2.3 I know that all my group identities are part of me—but that I am always ALL me.	Five Skills of Inclusion; Friendship Profile book
	JU.K-2.13 I know some true stories about how people have been treated badly because of their group identities, and I don't like it.	
You Can Play Too	AC.K-2.17 I can and will do something when I see unfairness—this includes telling an adult.	Friendly Musical Circles and Inclusion Role Plays using the Five Skills to Invite
	AC.K-2.19 I will speak up or do something if people are being unfair, even if my friends do not.	

The Empathy Puzzle

To help second graders understand the experiences of others, we begin by directly teaching about empathy. To help students to understand how empathy works, we share the five steps of empathy:

1. Look and Listen: What do their words say? What do their words sound like (tone of voice)? What does their body language say? What does their facial expression say?
2. Remember: Think about a time when you have felt the same way.
3. Imagine: Think about what you would feel like if the same thing happened to you.
4. Ask: Find out exactly how they feel by asking.
5. Care: Show them that you care about how they are feeling.

To complete the lesson, allow time for students to practice each of these steps of empathy. You can use role plays, sample vignettes, or practice in pairs.

Someone Else's Shoes

In this lesson, we practice empathy through the skill of inclusion. I begin with talking about how it feels to be left out. I relate to students with disabilities who may be excluded because of the differences. We watched a video from YouTube titled *Like Everyone Else: Learning Disability Awareness* (7 Stream Media, 2013). We then talked about reasons that people are excluded. The concrete example of disabilities helps students to understand the concept. While discussing exclusion and inclusion, make sure to ask students if people are ever excluded because of the color of their skin. Finally, practice what students can say or do to interrupt the act of students being excluded. Practicing the skill of interruption when you see something wrong is crucial for supporting students in stopping racism when they see it.

You Can Play Too

Now that students understand and have practiced the skill of empathy, it is time to further practice the skill of inclusion. We created five steps to inclusion:

1. Look around and notice: Is anyone being left out? Does anyone seem like they aren't having a good time?
2. Get the person's attention: Say hello, introduce yourself if you need to.
3. "Do you want to play with us?"
4. Explain what you are doing: Give the other student the information they need to join in.
5. Make sure they feel welcomed: smile, be friendly, actually include.

This lesson reminds me of the quote from Verna Myers: "Diversity is being invited to the party, inclusion is being asked to dance."

Third Grade Lessons

Title	Learning Objectives	Activity
Solutions, Solutions	JU.3–5.12 I know when people are treated unfairly, and I can give examples of prejudice words, pictures, and rules. AC.3–5.16 I pay attention to how people (including myself) are treated, and I try to treat others how I like to be treated.	Help the teacher think about the advantages and disadvantages people have in order to create an equitable classroom.
Strengths and Obstacles	ID.3–5.3 I can feel good about my identity without making someone else feel bad about who they are. DI.3–5.8 I want to know more about other people's lives and experiences, and I know how to ask questions respectfully and listen carefully and non-judgmentally.	Using superpower strengths to overcome obstacles—students will work collaboratively to create a product showing two people who use their strengths to overcome an obstacle.
What About Us	AC.3–5.17 I know it's important for me to stand up for myself and for others, and I know how to get help if I need ideas on how to do this. AC.3–5.20 I will work with my friends and family to make our school and community fair for everyone, and we will work hard and cooperate in order to achieve our goals.	Taking ownership and responsibility for inclusion in the school—a school map of inclusion. Students will create map as a class and then work in groups to create action plans for change in the major areas of the school where unfairness happens.

Solutions Solutions

In this lesson, we have a very confused teacher, I called her Ms. Muddled, who needs help in understanding how to create an equitable classroom. I start with the silly example of a broken egg on a counter (I use a picture but feel free to go big and actually break an egg, this would make a lasting memory). I ask students what solution could solve this problem. They answer a towel, a new egg, etc. I ask them "What if the solution I have is a pencil sharpener?" Of course, this is met with disbelief and laughter. We talk about how sometimes equity is what you need and not the same or equal item. I then give groups of students vignettes to read and solve for the confused teacher who needs help. The vignettes include students with special needs, students who are shorter or taller, and other very concrete needs.

Strengths and Obstacles

We all have strengths and obstacles. Sometimes children see strengths and obstacles as permanent or random. They might think that they aren't popular so they don't have influence. That they aren't smart so they can't learn. As adults, we are more adept at knowing that strengths and obstacles change over time and over effort. In this lesson, read a book from our diverse book list about people who overcome an obstacle. Watch a video about a paralympic athlete or an agent of social change. Show students strengths and obstacles. Finally, students will interview each other to determine what their strengths are. They will work with their partner to create a superhero of strength from the strengths they identify within themselves.

What About Us

At this point, our third graders have identified that equity is not the same as equality. They've identified their own strengths and the strengths of their classmates. Now it's time to let them move forward with action. Giving students a map of the school, allow them to work in groups to determine areas of action within your building. This is a book about racial equity, you say, what if they choose an area of action that is not related to race? I hold that the skill of action is the most important at this age. As long as this action comes from the whole of the group, and not just its dominant members, I think that building the capacity for action is necessary in the evolution of agents of change.

Fourth and fifth grade students are still solidly in the concrete operational stage of thinking. It's easy to assume that they are the oldest in the school and can understand the abstract but this is not yet a mastered skill. Students at this age are deeply connected to their friends. They enjoy being in groups but remain individualistic as well. This is a time when students begin to create subgroups of friends that are less and less fluid over time.

Fourth Grade Lessons

Title	Learning Objectives	Activity
What's Your Label?	ID.3–5.3 I know that all my group identities are part of who I am, but none of them fully describes me and this is true for other people too.	What is your label activity? Definition and discussion around vocabulary: Label, Assumption, Stereotype.
	JU.3–5.11 I try and get to know people as individuals because I know it is unfair to think all people in a shared identity group are the same.	

continued

Title	Learning Objectives	Activity
Social Activism Part 1	JU.3–5.25 I know about the actions of people and groups who have worked throughout history to bring more justice and fairness to the world.	Students will research historical social activists using a graphic organizer.
Social Activism Part 2	AC.3–5.19 I will speak up or do something when I see unfairness, and I will not let others convince me to go along with injustice.	Students will share their learning about social activism using creative methods.

What's Your Label?

We've all been labeled at some point. Sometimes we embrace this label, sometimes we reject it. However, no matter our response to the label, we are more than one descriptor. In this lesson, we explore the vocabulary of label, assumption, and stereotype. The activity for this lesson is one you've seen before—each person is given a label on their forehead or back that they cannot see. Others in the class must treat the person as their label describes. For example, if the label were angry, the class would act like the person was angry regardless of how the person acted. Everyone has a label and they must guess what their label is. At the end of the lesson, the class comes together in a circle to have an honest conversation about labels, assumptions, and stereotypes.

Social Activism

This lesson is in two parts. In the first lesson, students can learn about contemporary or historical social activists. I love the story of Jason Brown, an NFL player who quit at the top of his game to be a farmer who gives away all of his crops to food-insecure families. We discuss what he did and why. We talk about the criticism he would face and the obstacles that were in his way (he had never farmed). Once students can see a concrete example of activism with a relatable figure, we open up our research into more social activists.

In the second lesson, students actually begin researching social activists. I created a document with links to kid-friendly research sites and allowed groups of students to choose the activist they wanted to research. They answered three essential questions:

1. What are the words, behaviors, rules, and laws that treated people unfairly based on their group identities?
2. What were the actions taken to bring more justice and fairness to the world?
3. How can I speak up or do something when I see unfairness?

Once the groups researched their essential questions, they were asked to choose a creative way to share their learning. They could write a song/rap, make a short video, create a poster, design a presentation, or act in a role play. The idea was to take the almost-mythical examples of social activists like Malala Yousafzai, Ida B. Wells, or Cesar Chavez and make their stories relatable to the lives of fourth graders.

Fifth Grade Lessons

Title	Learning Objectives	Activity
Injustice in Bias	DI.3–5.7 I have accurate, respectful words to describe how I am similar to and different from people who share my identities and those who have other identities. AC.3–5.18 I know some ways to interfere if someone is being hurtful or unfair, and will do my part to show respect even if I disagree with someone's words or behavior.	Students will create posters to help others identify bias and act against it.
Understanding Race and Racism	JU.3–5.13 I know that words, behaviors, rules, and laws that treat people unfairly based on their group identities cause real harm. JU.3–5.14 I know that life is easier for some people and harder for others based on who they are and where they were born.	Students will research incidents of racism in history and the people who interrupted them.
What's Your Superpower?	DI.3–5.10 I know that the way groups of people are treated today, and the way they have been treated in the past, is a part of what makes them who they are. AC.3–5.20 I will work with my friends and family to make our school and community fair for everyone, and we will work hard and cooperate in order to achieve our goals.	Students will create their own superhero that uses the skills they possess to interrupt racism. They will work in groups to combine their superheroes into teams to create a fictional story of action based on assigned vignettes.

Injustice in Bias

If there is one thing that fifth graders can do, it is identify when something is unfair. "That's unfair" may be one of the most overused phrases in an upper elementary classroom. To capitalize on what students already believe, we explored the meaning of bias. To begin, ask students to draw a picture of a scientist, teacher, doctor, or nurse. One career at a time, ask students to stand if they drew a scientist and then continue standing if their scientist was a woman. As expected, most students drew the gender generally associated with that career, or a gender bias. We defined bias, stereotype, and injustice. Lastly, we showed advertisements (photo and video) of gender, race, religion, and culture bias. As a project, students worked together to create posters about recognizing bias.

Understanding Race and Racism

It's time for students to know the word racism and what it really means. I am hearing from many counselors in my district that students are calling each other racist even when the behavior does not mirror the accurate definition. I believe that many students understand that racism is bad but don't truly know what it means so may use the word to try to get others in trouble. In this lesson, we begin reading the poem "Growing in Harmony" by Xuan Duong. This poem is widely available on the internet. I chose the poem because it talks about harmony but clearly calls out race and racism as a disruptor of harmony. We asked students what harmony means and discussed that harmony involves at least two different sounds that work together to make something better. In our discussion of race and racism, I used the official Miriam-Webster dictionary definitions so that students, and other stakeholders, were clear that the definition was not influenced by my own bias. Finally, students spent time researching historical incidents of racism. I think it's important that they know that racism is much more than two students arguing on the playground. By using "racist" to describe interpersonal conflict between two people of a different race, we sever the word from its description of a deep and hurtful history of racial dominance and oppression.

What's Your Superpower

Adults learning about and experiencing bias and racism can feel overwhelmed by the enormity and helpless to make a change. Children are usually not so easily deterred. I wanted my students to feel empowered to make a change both within our school and in their lives in the community. In this lesson, we brainstormed a list of actions that students can take to interrupt racism and bias. Students were then tasked with creating their own superhero. This superhero would be their "alter-ego" that allowed them to use their strengths to do great things. Having access to art supplies so that they can really get into their creation is wonderful. It's amazing what they create. If you have time, allow them to work together to create teams of superheroes, à la Avengers, to fight against racism in simple vignettes.

Middle School

Middle school is characterized by massive changes for students. Physically, they may be experiencing puberty and growth spurts. The preteen brain also goes through physical development characterized by synaptic pruning and development of the prefrontal cortex (Caskey & Anfara, 2014). These brain shifts allow preteens to begin to develop the capacity for abstract thought. They are moving from concrete logical operations to acquiring skills to analyze and think reflectively. Middle-school students prefer active learning experiences and interactions with peers during educational activities. Because middle-school counselors can have more difficulty in accessing class time for social-emotional instruction, we created two lesson plans per grade at this level.

Sixth Grade Lessons

Title	Learning Objectives	Activity
Insta-Me	ID.6–8.1 I know and like who I am and can comfortably talk about my family and myself and describe our various group identities.	Create a "social media" profile with hashtags showing your interests. Include specific questions and topics to answer. Where is your family from, etc.
	DI.6–8.7 I know I am connected o other people and can relate to them even when we are different or when we disagree.	
Insta-You	JU.6–8.12 I can recognize and describe unfairness and injustice in many forms including attitudes, speech, behaviors, practices, and laws.	Students will share snap opinions about mock social media profiles, they will then discuss and share ideas for how snap decisions affect daily lives.
	AC.6–8.16 I am concerned about how people (including myself) are treated and feel for people when they are excluded or mistreated because of their identities.	

Sixth grade students are often moving into a new school and being introduced to new peers, new class structures, and increased social opportunities like clubs, school sports, and band. Sixth graders are really exploring who they are in a way that they may not have before.

Insta-Me

In a traditional elementary, middle, high system, sixth graders are entering a new school building and being introduced to students who may not have attended their elementary school. To help them to self-identify under the diversity domain of the Teaching Tolerance social justice standards, we created a Google slide template for an "Insta-Me" profile page. Instagram seems to be the most popularly used platform for the middle-school students in my area. If your students typically use a different platform, I recommend basing the lesson on that platform. In this template, students could share attributes about themselves, their families, and their culture. This allows students to celebrate their roots and to learn about others.

Insta-You

In this lesson, we created mock social media profiles of real people who defied stereotype. We would begin by showing only the "profile picture" and asked students to describe what they thought the person was like. The TED talk by Yassmin Abdel-Magied is a great accompanying video for students to watch (Abdel-Magied, 2014). In her talk "What does my headscarf mean to you?" she shares the bias and assumptions she faces. In reality, she is a slightly sarcastic race-car engineer. She is funny and relatable to students, I highly recommend her talk available on ted.com. The Mastercard commercial "Don't Judge a Book" is also a great accompaniment to this lesson.

Seventh Grade Lessons

Title	Learning Objectives	Activity
I Am but I Am Not	ID.6–8.3 I know that overlapping identities combine to make me who I am and that none of my group identities on their own fully defines me or any other person.	Read or listen to poem by Pat Mora *Legal Alien*. Students will create a visual or written representation of the "I am but I am not" counter-narrative.
You Are but You Are Not	JU.6–8.1 I relate to people as individuals and not representatives of groups, and I can name some common stereotypes I observe people using. AC.6–8.18 I can respectfully tell someone when his or her words or actions are biased or hurtful.	Students will watch the Ted Talk "Danger of a Single Story" and discuss stereotypes while focusing on the skills needed to hold difficult conversation.

Seventh graders are starting to identify with their middle-school selves. They've settled in a bit and are now beginning to look outward to what others are doing. They are starting to contemplate and possibly struggle with the narratives that others have assigned for them.

I Am (but I Am Not)

In this lesson, we want students to think about their own identity and identity groups that they may belong to—gender, race, religion, even sports, clubs, and other chosen identities. At the same time, we will explore the idea that all identities come with a story assigned by others, stereotypes, that may not be a part of who we are. This lesson will be hard for some students because they have not reflected on their identity so deeply before. It may be helpful to start with a brainstorm of all the identities that they relate to and then ask students to choose the one that other people most misunderstand about them. Finally, we want to turn their "I Am Not" into an "I Am." For instance, a student might say "I am a black male (identity group), I am not good at basketball (story assigned by others or stereotype)." They can then create their counter-narrative "I am a black male and I am great at science."

You Are but You Are Not

We are now ready to explore the stereotypes given to others and the way that these stereotypes can hurt relationships and our community. The lesson begins with watching all or part of the TED talk, "Danger of a Single Story," by Chimamanda Ngozi Adichie, where she talks about finding her own authentic cultural voice that includes many overlapping stories (Ngozi Adichie, 2009). Following the TED talk, students will use appropriate discussion skills to answer essential questions:

- What are some stereotypes you hear used about students in your school?
- Why do you think people use these stereotypes?
- How does the use of these stereotypes impact relationships between students in school?
- How can we respectfully tell someone when his or her words or actions are biased or hurtful?

The focus here is on more than these three questions but on the skills needed to hold high intensity conversations in a respectful and meaningful way. It's important to set ground rules before the conversation starts. Watch the time closely so that you have time to end the discussion with a debrief and to make sure that all students exit the classroom in a safe emotional space.

Eighth Grade Lessons

Title	Learning Objectives	Activity
Life Lessons and Our Stories	ID.6–8.2 I know about my family history and culture and how I am connected to the collective history and culture of other people in my identity groups. DI.6–8.9 I am curious and want to know more about other people's histories and lived experiences, and I ask questions respectfully and listen carefully and non-judgmentally.	Read excerpt from *Flying Lessons and Other Stories*, edited by Ellen Oh. Essential questions: • What is your race? • How did you come to learn what your race is? • What are positive/negative aspects of your race?
Squad Goals	JU.6–8.15 I know about some of the people, groups, and events in social justice history and about the beliefs and ideas that influence them. AC.6–8.20 I will work with friends, family, and community members to make our world fairer for everyone, and we will plan and coordinate our actions in order to achieve our goals.	Student Activism—research social activists, affinity groups, and student groups for positive change. Create an action plan for change within the school.

Eighth graders are the leaders of their building, they have become comfortable in their school and are often determined to change the world. To capitalize on this enthusiasm, we want to give them an opportunity to explore the concept of race, how it relates to them and others, learn about activism, and make a plan for action within the school. This is a big ask for two lessons. In one school in my district, the counselor worked with the social studies teacher to align anti-bias lessons with the social studies curriculum.

Life Lessons and Other Stories

In the book *Flying Lessons and Other Stories*, edited by Ellen Oh, well known children's authors share short stories that all have a protagonist that wants to be seen and validated. Each of the stories highlights different aspects of diversity, anti-bias, and typical dilemmas faced by kids. I recommend choosing a story that you think will most relate to your students. All will work with the essential questions of identity. Once identity has been explored, lead a discussion around race, learning about race, and the positive and negative aspects of one's own racial identity. Refer back to Chapter 4 and the questions you have already explored while self-reflecting. If time permits, prepare students for the next lesson by sharing stories of social activists.

Squad Goals

When I envision the school where I want my students and my own children to attend, I place a high level of importance on collaboration, acceptance, and activism. Squad goals means "what we want to be one day." So squad goals here allow students to envision the standard, "I will work with friends, family, and community members to make our world fairer for everyone, and we will plan and coordinate our actions in order to achieve our goals." The activities within the lesson will vary by school. If your school is highly socially active with affinity groups, support groups, and strong student leadership, you may need to do little explanation of social activism. Students will have the foundation they need to build an action plan for change based on their anti-bias learning. However, if this is a new skill set for your students, plan to spend time exploring what student activism could and does look like so that your students will have a model for their plans of action.

High School

Programming: Affinity Groups and Leadership Groups

School counselors are continuously in a position to influence change and be the leaders their school needs. "School counselors who understand instructional practices, especially those that support the school's vision and the standards of the time, create a counseling curriculum that is critical both to the school and to students' education" (Lopez and Mason, 2018).

Affinity, leadership groups, and comprehensive classroom lessons are a part of that curriculum in secondary schools. Affinity groups are defined as collective experiences shared by members of the same identity group. Many affinity groups exist on college campuses in such forms as the National PanHellenic Council and Black Student Unions. Gradually, secondary school programs are seeing the benefit of such organizations within their schools. Affinity groups, particularly for black students, are often a primary source of solace in an otherwise culturally refuting environment. This book is about inclusion—so how does one justify exclusion for the purpose of a social group? The black experience in high school, when students are developmentally solidifying their identity, can be reason to seek out commonality in the face of adversity. For example, the phenomenon of stereotype threat is highly visible in high-school and college students. Stereotype threat adds a cognitive burden that can lead to underperformance. Affirmation intervention, such as affinity groups, reduces physiological stress and makes people more open to uncomfortable information. When in a state of vigilance, as racial minorities may be when surrounded by a majority, people are less likely to focus on long-term goals and may perceive threats in ambiguous situations. Black students may find the affirmations needed to reduce the impact of this occurrence within an affinity group. The same reasoning is associated with Black Student Unions on predominantly white campuses.

The African American Male Achievement Program in Oakland Unified School District includes black male instructors teaching classes in manhood development. Ideas about black manhood are investigated with students. High-schoolers question more deeply cultural issues that affect them as individuals and their communities. The African proverb "I am because we are" is the basis of their group's understanding. Some schools have ventured to create white affinity groups for the sole purpose of understanding whiteness in America and dismantling racism. Groups such as this need to be carefully handled by experienced educators who can guide white students towards overall inclusivity and not perpetuate white supremacy.

From school council to the yearbook committee, leadership groups should be a reflection of the schools overall engagement. Anti-bias curriculum continues to be needed in high school. These lessons can be taught by the school counselor or included in advisory periods.

Ninth Grade Lessons

Title	Learning Objectives	Activity
Celebrating and Building Community	ID.9–12.4 I express pride and confidence in my identity without perceiving or treating anyone else as inferior.	"What's good?!" Share out guidelines, Celebrate, Reflect.
What are Social Skills?	DI.9–12.9 I relate to and build connections with other people by showing them empathy, respect, and understanding, regardless of our similarities or differences.	Article, Overview and video.
Digital Zombies Part I Part II	JU.9–12.11 I relate to people as individuals and not representatives of groups, and I can name some common stereotypes I observe people using. AC.9–12.18 I can respectfully tell someone when his or her words or actions are biased or hurtful.	Forehead Game, Debrief Digital Citizenship Activity, Reflect.
Valuing Education	ID.9–12.5 I recognize traits of dominant culture, my home culture and other cultures, and I am conscious of how I express my identity as I move between those spaces.	Agree to Disagree.

Celebrating and Building Community

Students should write something positive that happened to them during the past few weeks related to their identity. Be inclusive with identity characteristics such as a new high-school student, a white student, a trans student, a new big brother, etc. Provide definitions of identity if needed. Leave the positive up to interpretation, but appropriate to share in the school environment. Talk to students a bit about how reflection is going to be an important part in their transition into high school. Help students share guidelines on sharing out. Allow students the opportunity to pass if they do not wish to share aloud. Give each student 30 seconds to share their positive and how it impacted their week. Create a celebration for the day. Celebrations will continue throughout the day when students feel they need motivation. A celebration can be a chant "Go Ryan! Go Ryan!", a high-five, a special handshake, or a silly dance. Students should have input on what the celebration will be. Be sure students remember so they can engage each other throughout the school day. Practice with them how to celebrate each other. Also, take precaution that teachers and administrators are aware of each week's celebration so students will not be penalized. Finally, reflect on sharing with students. What was it like to think of a positive, recent, and identity-related memory? Was it easy or difficult? What was it like to share with friends?

What Are Social Skills?

This lesson includes brief lecture, a brief video, and an exit ticket. Explain in 5–10 minutes the meaning of social skills and relate that to ninth graders starting their high-school career as they further grow into their multiple identities. Find a culturally inclusive video showing students interacting. Ask students to identify what appears to be productive in the video and associate the behavior to a social emotional skill such as listening attentively, showing care to someone in need, or respectful discussion.

Add culturally fluent questions to lesson such as:

- Is listening attentively easier to do at school than at home? Why or why not?
- Without saying who, do you know of people who do not discuss respectfully?
- Is there ever a time when people should not be respectful of the discussion?
- What if someone says you are not a worthwhile person?
- Do you believe you can participate in that discussion respectfully or is it ok to leave the discussion altogether?
- When is it difficult to be socio-emotionally aware? What should happen when you are having a difficult time? What does it mean if you are having a tough time?"

Be thoughtful and intentional about selecting discussion questions that relate directly to your population and areas of growth and inclusivity. Keep in mind who is *not* in the group so that their voices might somehow be uplifted (such as a video with a person who uses a wheelchair or an undocumented student).

Digital Zombies

PART I

Provide a posterboard where students can list guidelines to digital citizenship. Digital citizenship includes ways students can have a positive social media presence, avoid plagiarism in assignments and decrease cyber-bullying. Once the guidelines are created, students play the "Forehead" game:

- Materials—cards premade with the name of someone famous or noteworthy the students will know. There should be two name cards for every student. (Names might include: Malala Yousafzai, Millie Bobby Brown, Cardi B, the principal, any teachers in the school, Marvel characters, Maya Angelou, etc.).
- Divide class into groups which should consist of four–six students with at least two groups in a workshop/class. Groups should form a small circle not too close to other groups.
- Each person in the group will get a card that they should NOT read. Place the card, name down, on each desk/floor mat. There should be the name of someone famous on every card, no two cards should be the same famous person. If you have three groups of five students, you should have at least 15 different famous people cards. At the start, the first player will raise the card (to their forehead) so their group members can see the name. The first player will then ask "Yes or No" questions to their group in order to discover who the name is. Group members can only answer yes or no and they do not have to agree.
- The winner is the first group to correctly name all the famous people on their group members' cards.

After this game, the group debriefs about the various ways in which they guessed the person. Students should highlight any characteristics that were especially helpful in guessing who someone is without knowing their name. Finally, discuss the people whose names were listed on cards. Why might students want to know these people?

PART II

Invite students to share their online and social media experiences. Refer back to the student-created guidelines of digital citizenship. Students should discuss any negative, harmful, or hurtful behavior they have ever witnessed on the internet. Students should then craft a letter of support and encouragement to any person who may have experienced cyber-bullying. This can be done in the form of a collective letter with everyone's signature. Students then outlines ways in which they will act as allies in the future. Be sure to troubleshoot allyship for students own self-protection.

Valuing Education

Place three signs around the room and make space for a lot of movement. The signs should be spaced enough so that students will have the ability to gather around the sign. The first sign reads "AGREE." The second sign reads "I NEED MORE INFORMATION"; students should be prepared to ask for the additional information they need. The third sign reads "DISAGREE." The school counselor reads a list of 10–15 statements about education. Quotes from notable figures might also prove helpful. Invite students to start in the middle of the room before the first statement is read. Students listen to the statement and decide whether they agree, disagree, or need more information. They should stand by the sign that is their choice. Allow time for students to share why they chose that sign. Statements should highlight race and difference such as "I believe all students have access to fair and equal education" or "The black students in our school are all on financial aid." Statements can be somewhat controversial because, again, high school is a time to take risks with complex thinking and understanding.

Tenth Grade Lessons

Title	Learning Objectives	Activity
Time Management	ID.9–12.3 I know that all my group identities and the intersection of those identities create unique aspects of who I am and that this is true for other people too.	Time Slots.
Tune In	ID.9–12.1 I have a positive view of myself, including an awareness of and comfort with my membership in multiple groups in society.	Music and Lyrics, Journal and Reflect.
	DI.9–12.8 I respectfully express curiosity about the history and lived experiences of others and exchange ideas and beliefs in an open-minded way.	

continued

Title	Learning Objectives	Activity
Grit	ID.9–12.5 I recognize traits of the dominant culture, my home culture, and other cultures, and I am conscious of how I express my identity as I move between those spaces.	Article, Discussion.
	DI.9–12.10 I understand that diversity includes the impact of unequal power relations on the development of group identities and cultures.	
	JU.9–12.12 I can recognize, describe, and distinguish unfairness and injustice at different levels of society.	
Managing Myself	JU.9–12.12 I can recognize, describe, and distinguish unfairness and injustice at different levels of society.	Accepted and Unaccepted expressions of anger.
	JU.9–12.15 I can identify figures, groups, events, and a variety of strategies and philosophies relevant to the history of social justice around the world.	
Step Your Game Up	ID.9–12.1 I have a positive view of myself, including an awareness of and comfort with my membership in multiple groups in society.	Article, Discussion, Course. Selection/Overview.
	AC.9–12.20 I will join with diverse people to plan and carry out collective action against exclusion, prejudice, and discrimination, and we will be thoughtful and creative in our action in order to achieve our goals.	

Time Management

Create a spreadsheet with time slots at the top of the page. Allow students five minutes to reflect on their identities and the ways in which they have multiple roles in their family, in school, and in the community. Allow students time to fill in the details of their day, including responsibilities related to their identity, such as: picking up siblings from school is an older sibling identity; babysitting relatives is a trusted family member identity; part-time work if they are of age is an employee identity; studying for class is a student identity; and sleep is part of human identity. Support students in exploring how to create more time for studying or homework, or pursuing clubs and sports. The underlying theme is to help students prioritize what will contribute to their growth as individuals. Students with a lot of "free time" can consider more involvement in communities of need. Students with little "free time" can consider getting help with responsibilities to focus on areas of growth. Practice with students how to ask for help.

Tune In

The message behind many pop and hip hop songs can be deciphered through an analysis of lyrics. First, assess the top ten popular songs in class from any genre and regardless of content. Teachable moments will arise from the lyrics regardless of what the artist intends. Post the lyrics of songs, using the censored version if necessary, on the walls of the classroom. "Round Robin" the songs with two students starting at each poster. Students will spend two minutes reading the lyrics and annotating responses, questions, thoughts, and feelings about what they read. After two minutes, students will rotate to the left until they have all annotated every song posted. The last round of "Round Robin" will be to share out with the group what has been annotated. Counselor will facilitate discussion about themes related to social justice, violence, relationships, and poverty/economics. Create relevant, thoughtful questions ahead of time, such as "What's the point of talking about these luxurious items when most people don't have them?"

Grit

Students are to read a short article about grit and how it does or does not offer them helpful solutions to their everyday struggles. Counselor will facilitate a discussion about the limitations of grit. Students will list five ways in which they all show resiliency—allow non-traditional answers. Students will list five ways in which they need their community's support to access resiliency. Students will then discuss ways in which they can support their peers during difficult moments.

Managing Myself

This involves further exploration of social-emotional skills, focusing on anger and body cues. Students will brainstorm signs of anger in themselves and in others, including facial expressions, words, thoughts, and actions. Students will spend time researching the expression of anger in another country such as Brazil, South Africa, and Korea. Students will then brainstorm reasons why people become angered, classifying anger into two categories (Accepted and Unaccepted). Counselor will give a distinction between the two. There can be a parking lot for circumstances that are unclear or need more discussion than time will allow. Students should be given time to reflect on their own signs of anger. Create a "channel" poster that can either be a river surrounded by grass or some variation of that visual. Students use colorful sticky labels to attach anger expressions to the grass area and attach positive outlets to the inside of the river. Get as artistic and creative as possible.

Counselor can also choose emotions that are representative of their school environment such as guilt, shame, and anxiety.

Step Your Game Up

Students will be led through a goal-setting activity with special focus on rigorous course planning. The term "achievement gap" will be introduced, led by students' ideas on what it means, how it came to be, and what they believe can be done about it. Discuss the definition of achievement gap with students and provide them any current statistics. *Teaching Tolerance* published an article about achievement and social mobility that states: "upward mobility for African Americans is relatively rare … differences between upward mobility between black and white Americans have remained consistent since 1880" (Reece, 2018, fifth para.). Ask students their thoughts on how and why the gap persists. Have students draw an action plan for themselves to help close the gap or uplift others. Give students time to brainstorm, collaborate, and finalize their list including but not limited to access to courses, programs, and opportunities. If the program students wish to have doesn't exist, assign a task force group to create it. Privileged groups should also discuss equity as it relates to sharing access.

Eleventh Grade Lessons

Title	Learning Objectives	Activity
Empathy	ID.9–12.4 I express pride and confidence in my identity without perceiving or treating anyone else as inferior.	A Mile in Her Shoes, Reflection.
	JU.9–12.15 I can identify figures, groups, events, and a variety of strategies and philosophies relevant to the history of social justice around the world.	
Conflict Resolution	DI.9–12.8 I respectfully express curiosity about the history and lived experiences of others and exchange ideas and beliefs in an open-minded way.	Let Them Fight, Reflection.
Decision Making	AC.9–12.17 I take responsibility for standing up to exclusion, prejudice, and injustice.	Buckets and Discussion.
Boundary Setting	ID.9–12.5 I recognize traits of the dominant culture, my home culture, and other cultures, and I am conscious of how I express my identity as I move between those spaces.	Lesson, Reflection, and then Practice, more reflection.
	AC.9–12.19 I stand up to exclusion, prejudice, and discrimination, even when it's not popular or easy or when no one else does.	

Title	Learning Objectives	Activity
Stress	ID.9–12.5 I recognize traits of the dominant culture, my home culture, and other cultures, and I am conscious of how I express my identity as I move between those spaces.	Mindfulness workshop.
Self-Advocacy	JU.9–12.14 I am aware of the advantages and disadvantages I have in society because of my membership in different identity groups, and I know how this has affected my life.	Lesson, Practice, Reflection.
Personal Statement	ID.9–12.2 I know my family history and cultural background and can describe how my own identity is informed and shaped by my membership in multiple identity groups.	College planning, reflections.

Empathy

Empathy is a muscle that must be exercised. Any opportunity to focus and practice compassion is incredibly important. Students will watch a short ten-minute movie clip featuring a range of emotion in predominantly people of color in a way that is not caricature. Have students write all the emotions they see during the video. Without the full context of the movie, ask students to share why someone might be experiencing these feelings. There are a limitless number of possibilities so allow students ample time to tackle each emotion. Have students write or share ways in which they can relate to the emotions of the video. See resource list in Appendix A for movie options.

Conflict Resolution

Pass out scenario cards to small groups. Each scenario should involve a conflict, of the kind illustrated in the boxed examples. Students should prepare an intervention or resolution to help the subjects in the scenario resolve the conflict. At the end of collecting solutions, ask the group how each scenario may or may not further impose danger on the students if all the students involved are from a marginalized community. Discuss and change solutions to include new options.

Example #1: Danesha and Tamara

During lunch, Danesha, Tamara, Lamore, and Kevin always sit together. On this particular day in early November, Tamara sits with a new student who she noticed ate alone yesterday. Danesha gets upset and tells Lamore and Kevin to ignore Tamara. Caught in the middle, Lamore and Kevin try to stay out of it but find themselves going between Tamara and Danesha sharing messages. The day before winter break, Tamara accidentally bumps into Danesha in the hallway and the two begin to shove each other. A teacher breaks it up and the two are sent to in-school suspension (ISS).

Example #2: Kyle and Kaleef

Kyle and Kaleef are joking around in class not paying attention to the lesson. Ms. Browder asks the boys to begin note-taking. The boys are teasing another student who has to use his sister's pink backpack as a replacement because his backpack straps broke. After class, Kaleef sneaks up behind the student and grabs his backpack, throws it to Kyle and the two boys run off down the hallway.

Decision Making

Create slips with phrases related to decisions. Slips should be in three categories: small, medium, and large decisions. Slips can be examples of decisions such as buying a house in a diverse neighborhood, choosing matching socks, telling an elder to not use the word "oriental" to label an Asian person, what to eat for dinner, intervening in a racist incident, attending a protest while on probation, and becoming a parent. Create 20–35 slips for each category. Label three buckets as small, medium, and large. Distribute slips to small groups. Allow the groups to choose a slip and discuss their thoughts on which bucket it belongs in and why. Students will then place the slip in that bucket. Allow time to reflect and discuss.

Boundary Setting

Give students a worksheet with three columns, titled Physical, Mental, and Spiritual, and ten rows. Counselor leads a ten-minute discussion on boundaries. Be sure students understand the definition. Students can then spend five minutes filling in the worksheet with their boundaries.

Students will then practice expressing their boundaries with others by pairing up and choosing two examples such as "My physical boundary is that I don't want to be touched by people I don't know. I will honor this boundary by assertively telling others to not touch me."

(My _____ boundary is _____. I will honor this boundary by _____.)

Time permitting, students will then switch to defend their partners boundary.

(My friend's boundary is _____. I need you to honor this boundary by _____.)

Stress

Mindfulness is often used in restorative justice practices to help students alleviate symptoms of stress. Lead a workshop of breathing meditation and gentle stretching, or bring a professional in to lead. Offer students a brief history of the evolution of yoga and meditation, including vinyasa and trap yoga as examples. This activity is especially helpful before and after testing.

Self-Advocacy

Divide students into teams. Each team should identify a social justice want or need for the school such as accessible honors courses, supply needs, or money for a sports team. Each team collaboratively drafts a proposal to get the need met. Counselor should create guidelines for each proposal such as who will benefit, if anyone will be at risk should the proposal be granted, why it's relevant to the community/school, which cause it will further if granted, how much it will cost, etc.

Each group will present to a panel of judges, invite a few teachers or administrators to participate. The judges will decide which group has the best proposal and give feedback to each team.

Personal Statement

As many students plan for the college admissions process, the personal statement or college essay, is a prime opportunity to collate the reflections of the past three high-school years. Students should be given time to choose one–three topics that respond to a Common App prompt. Each prompt is in some way related to identity. Students can reflect on their evolving identity as well how they are perceived, whether or not that perception is fair.

Twelfth Grade Lessons

Title	Learning Objectives	Activity
Hopes and Fears of Senior Year	ID.9–12.2 I know my family history and cultural background and can describe how my own identity is informed and shaped by my membership in multiple identity groups.	The Hope Tree.
"You good?!"	AC.9–12.17 I take responsibility for standing up to exclusion, prejudice, and injustice.	Discuss language and assimilation.
The Real World Parts I and II	AC.9–12.20 I will join with diverse people to plan and carry out collective action against exclusion, prejudice, and discrimination, and we will be thoughtful and creative in our actions in order to achieve our goals.	Building Bridges and Career Day.

continued

Title	Learning Objectives	Activity
The Culmination	ID.9–12.1 I have a positive view of myself, including an awareness of and comfort with my membership in multiple groups of society.	Who I Was–Who I Am individual project and speech.

Hopes and Fears of Senior Year

Students continue to goal-set and plan for their academic, social, and emotional wellbeing throughout their academic career. Seniors should also reflect on current events that may affect their last year of high school. Create a hope tree with the assistance of talented artists in the building. Have seniors add sticky labels to the tree and display in a public space at school along with pictures of the seniors (with permission). Seniors might also begin to collect family information about parents' and grandparents' experiences transitioning out of high school.

"You Good!?"

Exploring the use of language in various settings, the school counselor will work with students to examine code-switching. Counselor will define code-switching with students and facilitate students' response to the following question: Which language should we use and why? Students then share ideas about how language use is representative of culture. Introduce ideas about assimilation, cultural appropriation, and cultural fluency into the conversation. Be prepared with questions such as "Why do you believe people feel pressure to assimilate?" and "How can people show appreciation for diversity without being offensive?"

The Real World I and II

PART I

Have students answer the following question: How is our school different from the world beyond our school walls? Students list all of the differences they observe on giant poster pages. Build bridges with students. This can be done in art form, written form, or through discussion and note-taking. Help students to bridge school learning and behaviors to "the real world." For example, taking AP courses might bridge to attending a well-networked business program. Another example is how learning to resolve conflict in high school might bridge to good relationships with co-workers.

PART II

Career Day introduction to diversity in the workplace, in the community, and on college campuses. Each student should prepare a question to ask a career-day presenter as it relates to inclusion within the workforce. It is helpful to give the presenters forewarning about the nature of questions some students might ask.

The Culmination

Identify formation reflection speeches are written by all students and shared by students who choose to do so. Students spend a week or more crafting speeches they will share with the class about how they have grown as a person using multiple labels and identities. Students will include how their high-school experience helped shaped their identity and how they will choose to better the lives of others who may or may not share their identity using concrete action plans. Seniors should create a plan to share their speeches with grades 9–11 in a celebratory setting.

See List of Resources in Appendix A for additional materials and support for these activities

Individual and Group Counseling

It seems remiss to discuss student activities without mentioning the profound work of school counseling in individual and group counseling for students. When working with children of color, it is imperative that school counselors have the skills necessary to understand the context in which students live and to effectively broach the topic of race, equity, bias, and social justice with students. We recommend the 2018 article from the International Journal of Advanced Counseling titled *Getting Comfortable with Discomfort: Preparing Counselor Trainees to Broach Racial, Ethnic, and Cultural Factors with Clients during Counseling* for those interested in diving deeper into this topic (Day-Vines, Booker Ammah, Steen, & Arnold, 2018).

For students of color, race, equity, bias, and social justice may come with negative experiences or even trauma. Recent work in the area of trauma-informed schools and trauma-informed care has been promising in supporting students who have experienced trauma. Recently, the idea of Healing Centered Engagement has risen to the forefront as a strength-based approach for those who have experienced trauma (Ginwright, 2018). In this approach, practitioners work to strengthen emotional literacy so that children can share their experiences and emotions to build empathy with young people. Students can then dream and imagine to see beyond the event or circumstance that caused trauma while building critical reflection to examine their response to trauma. Young people are encouraged to take action to change the circumstances that have led to their trauma, for example, fighting child abuse, protesting gun laws, or promoting programs that fight to end food insecurity. This action is a part of the healing process and builds a sense of power and control in their lives.

From the earliest stages of life to the transitions into college and career, school counselors are at the forefront of leading students toward a life of justice and peace. What are we doing if we are not cultivating the kinds of students who can continue to make the world safer for all?

References

7 Stream Media. (2013, November 1). *Like Everyone Else—Learning Disability Awareness*. [Video File]. Retrieved from https://youtu.be/Q2PIizndq-g.

Abdel-Magied, Yassmin. (2014, December). *What Does My Headscarf Mean to You?* TED: Ideas Worth Spreading, TEDxSouthBank. Retrieved from www.ted.com/talks/yassmin_abdel_magied_what_does_my_headscarf_mean_to_you.

Caskey, M., & Anfara, V. A., Jr. (2014, October). *Developmental characteristics of young adolescents.* Retrieved from www.amle.org.

Day-Vines, N. L., Booker Ammah, B., & Steen, S. (2018). Getting comfortable with discomfort: Preparing counselor trainees to broach racial, ethnic, and cultural factors with clients during counseling. *International Journal for the Advancement of Counselling, 40,* 89.

Ginwright, S. (2018, May 31). The future of healing: Shifting from trauma informed care to healing centered engagement. *Medium.* Retrieved from https://medium.com/@ginwright/the-future-of-healing-shifting-from-trauma-informed-care-to-healing-centered-engagement-634f557ce69c.

Lopez, C., & Mason, E. (2018). School counselors as curricular leaders: A content analysis of ASCA Lesson Plans. *Professional School Counseling, 21*(1b), 1–12. American School Counselor Association.

Ngozi Adichi, Chimamanda. *The Danger of a Single Story.* TED: Ideas Worth Spreading, TED-Global2009, July 2009. Retrieved from www.ted.com/talks/chimamanda_adichie_the_danger_of_a_single_story.

Oh, E. (2017). *Flying lessons and other stories.* New York: Crown Books for Young Readers.

Reece, R. L. (2018). Debunking the mobility myth. *Teaching Tolerance.* Retrieved from www.tolerance.org/magazine/spring-2018/debunking-the-mobility-myth.

Teaching Tolerance Curriculum Training Workbook. (2017). Southern Poverty Law Center.

Vittrup, B. (2015, July 6). How silence can breed prejudice: A child development professor explains how and why to talk to kids about race. Retrieved from: www.washingtonpost.com/news/parenting/wp/2015/07/06/how-silence-can-breed-prejudice-a-child-development-professor-explains-how-and-why-to-talk-to-kids-about-race/?noredirect=on&utm_term=.28b717dc43b2.

Chapter 6

The Benefit of Staff Reflection
The Work Continues With Everyone

Counselors have a unique opportunity to lead the charge and create opportunities for staff, students, and families to learn about their own personal bias and how their biases impact school culture and student life. Self-reflection activities allow counselors the space and information necessary to self-evaluate, self-correct, and be more open to feedback that can help us improve our practices. We have to remain open to hearing how we affect others because our daily interactions can greatly impact the lives of our students. There is a saying that educators can either nurture or traumatize children. We must not only know the difference but we must act as if nurturing children is our only option.

We have tapped into activities that allow us to explore our families, our upbringing, our relationships with students, our relationships with other educators, and our philosophies as school counselors. As we fully embrace reflection and change, we take into account the system in which we work. The education system has a history. The history of our education system is ripe with successes and failures. By learning from those successes and failures we can continue to build upon what works and improve what is harmful to faculty and students. In Chapter 1 we reviewed some of the history of education so that we can better understand where we are today and what we need to do differently to maintain steady progress. Some might argue that we are not progressing fast enough, that change needs to be immediate to save future generations from the failures of the past. Whatever your pace, rely on the support systems that exist to help you achieve your personal, and professional, goals. The system of education is a mighty one—from the Department of Education to your local school board. When you feel as if your small, singular person, school counselor voice is not heard, remember and know that we are advocates for ourselves and the profession. There are thousands of school counselors across the world that want the same outcome as you.

The Education System

We start with the system as a whole so that school counselors can gain perspective of a broad and all-encompassing institution. Improving our understanding of the education system as a whole helps us to better understand our role as we operate within the system. The education system functions on a federal level, the foundation of education is covered by this system. Laws are in place to protect students' and families' rights. We are most often confronted with laws that relate to special

education, Title I funding, or female students and sports. These laws are a spe-
cialty of educational lawyers who spend years and years in law school focusing on
education. Does this mean we don't find fault in federal laws that govern our
schools or the absence of laws where students need protection? No. For every
law that currently exists, there was once no law. Something happened for behaviors and practices to be deemed illegal. Black students were legally prohibited
from attending white schools. Female students were legally prohibited from
joining certain academic clubs and organizations. Laws often evolve and change
alongside the morality of society. Our educational laws are in place to help
govern our behavior and we can better understand them when we become
directly involved with their implementation.

As complex and daunting as it may occasionally be for counselors and educators
to think of the overall system of education, there are people who stand up to our
system. There are people who critique our system. There are people who question
our system. If we commit to embracing our social justice lens, we can view the
system of education as one that has long been like most of the institutions in the
United States—negatively impacting the lives of people of color. This is a bold
statement to make because, obviously, many black and brown students vehemently
pursue education. Many black and brown students persist in educational settings.
More than ever in history, black and brown students achieve college graduation
and careers in fields that help the country and thus the world. Realistically, and as a
counter to students of color that thrive, the achievement gap has not narrowed.

Our definition of racism includes an operative word—disproportionately. To
be a racist education system means that, overall, our education system at a federal,
state, and local level, disproportionately and negatively impacts the lives of people
of color. We can extend that to say LGBTQ students, immigrant students, and
students with disabilities. The National Center for Education Statistics (U.S.
Department of Education, 2018) reports an overall 12 percent difference between
white and black student graduation rates. Once we can accept this fact as our
present reality and remove the biases that suggest this difference is hereditary, we
can be active against what hurts our students.

Let's look at an event occurring in Baltimore, Maryland as an example of a
public school receiving federal, state, and local funding to operate (*Baltimore Sun*,
2018). Baltimore city schools rely on government and tax dollars to function.
Property taxes contribute to money that schools use to operate. Naturally, low-
income areas cannot contribute to children's education nearly as much as affluent
areas. On the coldest days of the 2018 winter, Baltimore City school buildings are
literally crumbling under the frigid conditions. Areas such as Potomac, Maryland,
where the median home is valued at $855,000, are not reporting any heating or
building issues at their local schools. Does this mean every public school in Baltimore city is falling apart? Absolutely not, but when we compare, across the
country, which public schools are disproportionately and negatively impacting the
lives of students we are consistently left with the same result. As of today, there is
no federally mandated law that exists to make funding equitable throughout each
state despite the gaps in wealth. Reflect on the following questions:

- How much do you know about the impact of federal and state laws at your
  school?

- How can you gain general information in this area? Who can you talk to?
- Are there activist organizations in your community that bridge the Department of Education and your local school district?

Institutional Systems Level Reflections

Get politically Involved or at the Very Least Become Aware

Let's proceed with a lens toward human ecology. The macrosystem is the area that surrounds the students' life in a way that is the "biggest picture." As a nation governed by federal laws, the rules of the land influence the ways in which we ultimately govern our student body. As a larger societal system, learning the details of how your school operates under and is affected by the federally dictated Department of Education is a direct way of disrupting racism.

Know Your Context

Understanding

We explored the context of our families and our own personal histories. We related this information to why we became educators and school counselors. We created art, notes, family trees, books, and other ways of documenting how we came to be. We also had a very brief introduction to how education came to be what we now know it as. Schools are legally allowed to integrate, though many do not. Public and private education alike are profoundly segregated by race. The laws that govern our country provide rules for what is permitted. Enforcement of these rules are a different story.

Activities

Question society's value of education and more specifically integrated education.

- What thoughts and ideas come to mind?
- What evidence do you have of these ideas?
- Write down your thoughts and questions generated from these questions.

Recall the origins of Brown v. Board of Education 64 years ago. Many of the elementary and middle school students at that time are still alive.

- What thoughts and ideas come to mind about how that generation of people view integration and other issues of education and race?
- Do you believe values change drastically by geographic region?
- How do you believe your geographic region views education and race today in comparison to 1954? Write down what comes to mind.

Create a "political tree." Start with the United States Secretary of Education and include the names and positions of key official stakeholders down to your administration. Add information or quotes from each person about their views of education. If any have offered views about the achievement gap and/or race-relations, include those quotes too. Step back and reflect on the climate illustrated in your tree.

Take Inventory (Federally and Locally)

Understanding

Forming your thoughts and ideas about the context in which we counsel students will lend itself to the actions we take to further advocate for what is necessary. Taking inventory challenges the school counselor to make note of a number of decisions that affect students. The decisions could be made at the federal level, such as Title IX, or at the local level, such as access to career day funding. Similar to what might be done in a small classroom library, leadership must see what is present and what is missing. Leadership must then create a plan to incorporate the missing into school program. This can be challenging work: how does one know what they don't know? Some deeper examination may be required. We recommend researching schools who are "getting it right" as presented in Chapters 1 and 7.

Many schools implement strategies to address gaps in access and achievement. Researching "gap-fillers" can lead counselors to view exemplary schools. A quick internet search of race-related bullying interventions or Black History Month celebration ideas can generate, at the very least, clues for closing the gaps that exist at your school. The same quick search can also generate ideas about socially unacceptable interventions and behaviors like black-face and cultural appropriation. There are schools across the country that have successfully learned to fill in the gaps of the needs of their school communities. Get in the habit of *not* reinventing the wheel and duplicating, with relevant amendments, what works for your population.

Activity

Ask yourself and/or colleagues the following questions:

- What laws are in place that regularly surface as an issue within your school?
- In what ways did your school leadership adapt Every Student Succeeds Act?
- Knowing education laws change with the administration, what struggles does your school experience that directly relate to federal law?
- Is your racially diverse school excluding marginalized groups from access to athletics, gifted programs, or AP classes?

By no means are we suggesting counselors become educational lawyers. We are encouraging counselors to have an idea of the ever-changing laws that affect our policies and programs. For example, Washington, DC provides a special program for residents of the district to apply for funding for college.

The DC Tuition Assistance Program (DCTAG) was created by Congress in 1999 by the District of Columbia College Access Act; PL 106–98 and amended by DC College Access Improvement Act 2002 and DC College Access Improvement Act 2007 for the purpose of expanding higher education choices for college-bound residents of the District of Columbia. All public institutions, Historically Black Colleges and Universities (HBCUs), and private nonprofit colleges and universities within the Washington Metropolitan area are eligible to participate in the DCTAG. The DCTAG expands higher education choices for District residents by providing grants of up to $10,000 toward the difference between in-state and out-of-state tuition at public colleges and universities (two-year and four-year) throughout the US, Guam and Puerto Rico. DCTAG also provides up to $2,500 per academic year toward tuition at private colleges in the Washington, DC Metropolitan area and private Historically Black Colleges and Universities (HBCUs) nationwide. Currently DCTAG has students in attending over 300 colleges and universities.

(Office of the State Superintendent of Education, D.C., 2018)

In essence, the district has realized a need for financial equity because state college systems are generally a less expensive means to obtain a college education. The program is available because the district, unlike any other area of the country, does not have a state college system. The DC grant offers students additional money to cover out-of-state tuition. A recent presidential budget proposal suggested cancelling this funding for students. How is this an issue of race? The majority of low-income DC students who benefit from this grant are African-American/black and Latino. If the program were to end, high schools would need to create solutions to close this additional gap in financial aid access. School leaders began a swift and direct advocacy campaign using social media, petitions, calling senators, and visits to the Capitol to demand the program continue. They were informed and organized in their response to the potential cut of this program. They were relentless in their efforts and they knew who to contact to advocate for students.

These educator activists achieved their goal and the program remained for another budget year. They knew their political context, they took inventory of this important funding source and they took action.

- What is happening in this country related to race? How is that related to education?
- What is happening in my school that relates to race? If you don't know, ask others. If others don't know, bring in a professional to assist you in taking inventory of the issues, gaps, and possible missteps.

Know Your Representation

Understanding

The individuals who represent our federal government, state-level government, local government, and our schools operate within sets of beliefs. Knowing who is in charge will help you not only identify gaps but also how many of the rules that exist came to be. Keep in mind, only 60 years ago, governing bodies believed white children and black children should not learn together. Today, we may think that belief is archaic. What we fail to realize, when separating ourselves from evils of the past, is that 60 years from now, we will be viewed as archaic. Progress undoubtedly involves some level of activism.

Activity

Refer to your "political tree." Ask yourself and/or a colleague these questions:

- Do you have a local school board? Who is on that board?
- Are you led and influenced by a Board of Trustees? Who is on that board?
- What beliefs does your mayor, senator, governor hold about education? How do their beliefs affect your students?

This will aid in your being able to connect with local officials on advocacy issues. Connecting the inventory or needs of the school to those who hold the power to influence those needs is crucial. Social media is a wonderful avenue to start searching for your representatives. We can see updated statements and comments of our elected officials in real time. Follow the people who make decisions for your school. Know who they are and how to connect with them. Remember to remain professional. Connecting to officials via social media offers a more casual avenue to interact but we should hold ourselves to a standard knowing that our comments are public for anyone to view.

In 2014, what started as a small group of teachers and counselors became a large force of policy-changing motion in Philadelphia, PA. The Caucus of Working Educators formed a group in response to shifts in local governing many thought were plagued with racist ideology (Caucus of Working Educators, 2018). The group worked diligently for years attending meetings, organizing protests, recruiting educators, and mobilizing through social media to disrupt their local system. These actions often start with a few people's ideas and can gradually develop into groundbreaking change. The Caucus of Working Educators isn't alone. There are organizations throughout the country that start locally and gradually work to improve the lives of students across the nation. With our latest director of the Department of Education having no in-class experience, no experience managing a school, no experience managing school-related budgets, and no experience managing anything related to education equity issues, it can be argued the mere appointment of such a candidate disproportionately and negatively affects the lives of students of color. So what do we do? We do not have the power to fire the director of the Department of Education. What we do have is numbers. The number of educators (teachers and counselors combined) will always outweigh the number of administration on every level. We can highlight the leverage we have in working together to help anyone and everyone understand the daily plight of our most vulnerable students.

School-Wide Systems Level Reflections

We have introduced the concept of the audit and encouraged you to take inventory of the political landscape in your community, state, and the nation. Let's shift our focus to our school's landscape. You may have skimmed the surface of your school's physical appearance, the clubs you offer, the paintings on the walls, and the events you plan. As a school counselor, you know the direct impact school policies have on discipline and school culture. We now have an idea of the laws that inform school policy. We know from reading and interacting with local politicians that the government's reach is only but so far. Our school leadership continues what our federal leadership began. While the Director of the Department of Education cannot make a policy about clothing choices in school, our individual principals and vice principals can. Our heads of school and deans can.

School Wide Policies Audit

Reflect on seemingly innocuous policies that many schools create with the good intention of protecting its student body.

Hiring Educators Who Are Familiar and/or Within Current Staff's Professional Circle (Hughes, 2014)

Educators know other educators. Networking is a great way of hiring someone who is already known and vetted as being an appropriate choice for the school's available position. Why might this be detrimental to students of color? Studies show that people belonging to a particular race will likely know and befriend others from that same race. According to the Public Religion Research Institute, the average white American has one black friend out of 91 friends (Cox, Navarro-Rivera & Jones, 2016). Today, most teachers are white and female regardless of the population their school serves. Hiring practices need to become more inclusive and represent the students within the school and surrounding community. Further, a diverse faculty is important even if our entire student body is white. Research suggests that an inclusive faculty is more beneficial than a homogenous faculty (Howard, 2016). Students learn the nuances of culture, language, and difference when they are surrounded by diversity. The world that we hope our students will someday explore is incredibly diverse, trusting the experiences of people different from you increases your capacity to empathize. We have included questions to ask during hiring interviews at the end of this chapter to shift your leadership's thinking using a social justice lens.

Interrupt faulty hiring practices with interviewing questions that focus on diversity (as listed by J. Piperato):

- How have you been educated to understand the history of black and brown folks in the United States?
- Why are some folks poor in the United States?
- What has afforded you the privilege and power to sit before us today and how will it impact your role in this position?
- In what ways, have you/could you perpetuate systems of oppression in education and what are you actively doing to stop this from happening?
- What is the opportunity gap and how do you hope to address it at this institution?

- What is white privilege and how is it perpetuated in education/school counseling?
- How would you define social justice and what role has it played in your past positions? Please be specific.
- How would you cultivate an environment that works to dismantle inequities for marginalized populations?
- Please describe a bias that you have and how you are working to overcome it.
- Please describe a time when you had to alter or change non-inclusive behavior/language in your own life. Why did you change and what did the process look like?
- What are three techniques you use to ensure you are using a social justice lens when planning an event?
- Describe how you would center the experience of marginalized students in your role.
- As a faculty member, what are three areas that you will focus on while in this position to close the opportunity gap for black and brown students? Be specific to what you would do in those three areas.
- Please describe an experience where your privileged identities impacted your ability to connect to a marginalized student (in your past roles).

Students and Faculty May Not Wear Hair Styles or Clothing That is Distracting to Learning

Learning is optimal when students can attend to the content in ways that further their understanding. Distractions interrupt learning. Why might this policy be detrimental to students of color? Much like the practice of law in our society, our biases affect the way rules are enforced. Distracting hair and clothes are subjective. With reports pouring into the media about black female students being suspended because of their braided extensions or afros, one must question whether or not this policy disproportionately and negatively affects black girls. Policies are created to keep students safe without regard to enforcement. Counselors must collaborate with disciplinarians, deans, and administration to assess how policies are enforced and who is affected by the policy. Notice proportions as they pertain to your overall student body and the number of students negatively affected by a policy. If a distracting hair policy is suspending 10 black girls a year and 2 white boys a year but there are only 25 black girls and 100 white boys in the entire school, the policy is disproportionately affecting black girls. If your political protest policy suspends 1 black boy a year and no one else even though 250 students participated in some form of political protest during the school year, the policy and/or the way it's enforced may be racist. Take the time to create an accurate and true report based on policies and enforcement of rules in your school. The report should include a response to the findings such as: "Given this data, we recommend a re-evaluation of how we suspend students based on the policy. Options include parent conferences to avoid suspension proactively, rewriting the policy to exclude hairstyles, providing seating charts that negate the opportunity of distraction…". Creativity and flexibility is our goal, rigid and inflexible policies that cause more harm than good can no longer be supported.

Students Must Resolve Conflict Civilly

No educator wants fist fights to occur between students. We know that violence is devastating as it puts our students in physical danger. We must, however, become more nuanced in our interpretation of violence as a means to control versus violence as the body's response to danger. In other words, a fist fight to stop a peer from talking about his/her mother versus a fist fight out of fear a peer will harm a younger sibling. In our attempts to keep all students physically safe, we have made sweeping generalizations about violence. We suspend any student who raises their fist without understanding the context of their behavior. For example, in our attempts to appease parents looking from the outside in, as policy, we expel the angry child who slams their fist on the desk and throws their assignment in the trash. The context we lack is that no child should have to sit through a mock "slave auction" and be expected to not become blind with rage (Mazzola, 2017). Imagine that detention explanation to a 9 year old: "Despite your anger and humiliation, banging the desk is not allowed, so you are hereby punished."

Some rules are insensitive and potentially further damaging if they are disseminated without context. Imagine two students being placed in the same class who have a history of racial tension and leaders expect one to not boil over with emotion. This sets the standard that children are to not behave as young, growing human beings who make mistakes. Our definition of civility must take into account the range of human emotion and reaction. Physical violence of any kind remains unacceptable, but instead of "zero tolerance" policies that do not address underlying concerns, we suggest adopting "context-savvy" approaches that differentiate between equality and equity. We are also skilled enough to find the language to communicate our disciplinary actions to families so they, too, feel safe and protected.

Furthermore, as we examine our policies and implementation patterns, we must take precaution as it pertains to the school to prison pipeline. The National Education Association is clear in stating:

> the school-to-prison pipeline disproportionately places students of color, including those who identify as LGBTQ, have disabilities, and/or are English Language Learners, into the criminal justice system for minor school infractions and disciplinary matters, subjecting them to harsher punishments than their white peers for the same behaviors. The school-to-prison pipeline diminishes their educational opportunities and life trajectories. All educators—which includes every school employee—are key to ending the school-to-prison pipeline.
>
> (National Education Association, 2016, Introduction)

The over-enforcement of policies against students of color is directly related to biases educators hold of those students. By confronting and shifting your biases, you become a better advocate for your students. You protect your students the way all children deserve to be protected.

Counselors can increase their skills in restorative justice practices and healing communities that include solutions to concerns, not punishments that may lead to more danger for students of color. Proactively troubleshoot why this may be logistically difficult for you. With a study body of over 1,000 students and only one, two, or three counselors, case-by-case involvement can seem even more daunting. We are tasked with two primary responsibilities: (1) To do our very best to remain case-by-case sensitive and "context-savvy," and (2) To advocate for the appropriate number of counselors in your school. We know this is a challenge. We know it is an ongoing struggle for most education professionals. Our hope is that with the growing movement of student-led organizations calling for peaceful responses to violence, including less school police officers and more school counselors, the changes will soon be accepted as normalcy.

Identifying what is happening on a daily basis within your school is key. What do you do about these rules? Knowing that the school rules and policies affect everyday student life, you must act. We suggest that counselors record the rules and policies if they are not already displayed. Critique them. This can be an annotated activity on a lazy Sunday afternoon while sipping sweet tea on your front porch. This activity can be the last 30 minutes of your Friday before you begin your self-care enriched weekend. Pull discipline records of students who were affected by these policies and rules. Be sure to write those instances down to support your understanding. If you are in a position to delegate this task to the dean and/or disciplinarian, do so. We even encourage discussing your thoughts and observations with a loved one. Sometimes, someone else can help you better grasp the accuracies or fallacies of your ideas. Discuss the incidences within your counseling team or with other student support services colleagues. Next, plan how you will bring the findings to the school leadership meetings and your school counseling advisory council. What can be helpful is if you have added agenda items before your next meeting. Ask your principal if you can present a concern about student experiences in school. Create the meeting if space does not already exist.

Ask your principal for 30 minutes of their time to discuss the student recently suspended for wearing a "Free Meek" t-shirt (Willingham, 2018). Be prepared for that meeting, anticipate pushback, and practice what you will say. Come ready to offer a solution. Administrators are solving problems all day. Let's take the initiative, as we often do, in finding solutions to our schools race problems. Find allies in your school to aid you in making your school as anti-racist as possible. Involve families. Create learning opportunities for all. School counselors love professional development that not only applies to teachers but is useful for any educator who works with and for students. Professional development is a way to reach all educators and administrators in a manner that seeks to arrive at one mission, one goal, or one purpose.

Counselor–Colleague Systems Level

As holders of systemic power, being the leader in another system can provide both anxiety and a sense of urgency. When white counselors are educated and aware of race-related issues, they can and should use their privileges of whiteness and professional leadership position to improve conditions for all students in various ways. School counselors of color are able to reflect on the dynamic they have with colleagues to better inform their practice. We can identify key ways in which you can start impacting the system within your faculty regardless and in spite of your identity.

Have conversations with your colleagues about race. When doing so, label your identities. "As a white man who works in a leadership position at my school, I want to be knowledgeable about how these issues today affect my students." Such a declaration promotes a clear understanding of your perspective and it also helps everyone listening consider their identity as it relates to their professional responsibilities. This is a clear and concise way of using your privilege to promote change. Yet, statements as simple as the one listed above can evoke a sense of anxiety and fear. Many still consider the mention of race to be rude, improper, or even unprofessional. These are barriers to the work of socially conscious education and school counseling.

Be aware of the context in which you work. Is your school community avoidant of race? Does your community even acknowledge privilege? Schools may need gradual guidance towards the use of contemporary language and ideas. There is lingering anxiety about labels. Many communities no longer use the term "African-American." Young adults today use "black" and "white" far more often than "African-American" and "Caucasian." Gauging the temperature of your environment will help you find the words to describe the areas of growth your school may need. You may discover that the statement above is the first time anyone in the meeting refers to themselves as white. There is utility in language choice.

Let's take a look at an example. A school counselor in a leadership team meeting listens as the principal describes a family as African-American and poor while associating these characteristics to social problems in school. Again, label your identities.

> As a white female middle-class school counselor, I would want to be careful of the associations I make to race and socioeconomic opportunities. We are a majority white school which can have a different, at best, difficult, at worst, meaning for our black students.

At a national conference several years ago, we were confronted with this very situation during our session about interrupting racism. A counselor approached us after our presentation and explained how she felt uncomfortable facilitating a conversation about race and class as a middle-income white woman. In these moments, the building bridge is acknowledgment of one's privileges. Introduce your relevant identities into the conversation. At the opposite end of the spectrum, some counselors will find they are behind the curve. More progressive communities have been using the language and exploring the ideas for decades—this work is not new, in the sense that race and education have been studied since the 1800s. Consider the assignment of "playing catch-up." Counselors who are learning and integrating into schools and communities already highly aware of race relations might benefit from the comprehensive and thorough exploration of every activity in this book. We have to be prepared to own our privileges in order to honestly confront student lives with our biases. We all have biases—some counselors are blind to the ways in which they view the world and difference. The argument can be made that a counselor who is blind to their biases is unable to attend to the needs of their students in comprehensive, beneficial, and complex ways. This offers further rationale to why counselors must continuously confront the histories, perspectives, and worldviews we bring into our schools and onto our leadership teams.

Professional development (PD) gives school faculty the opportunity to fine tune their practice. Designed to supplement graduate school education, professional development across sectors is a way for professionals to stay connected to and gain further information and skills from what aids in our growth and understanding. Our work benefits from professional development. All professional development, however, is not beneficial. A common concern of school counselors at every level is that professional development within schools does not pertain to us. We understand. When there are 100 teachers in a building and 1 counselor, the likelihood that the PD will focus on counselor needs is slim. All the while, we still need to remain current and relevant within our practice. Part of the professional development work is resourcing and funding speakers. Resourcing activities is a testament to the priorities of the institution. As a function of economic racism, people from communities of color are often left with a burden to educate others for free while university professors (typically white and male) are salaried for the exact same lessons. These burdens are unfair and an extension of economic racism so it is important that if educators want to learn about how racism impacts their school community, they hire people belonging to those communities to teach them. Of course, this will not always be an option. Race researchers and speakers who travel the country offering professional development belong to all races. Schools should seek the person or people who can give their staff what they need. Schools should also be mindful of how these complexities contribute to or fight against racism overall. Many white social justice activists work for free or donate their proceeds to nonprofit organizations. Such factors should be considered. The most important factor is for schools to invite the professionals that will meet their faculties' needs.

As it relates to race and socially conscious school counselors, many opportunities for professional development already exist. Local divisions of school counselor associations often include diversity and inclusion sessions at their annual conferences. Get involved. The speakers who lead those sessions are great resources. They typically have studied issues related to equity or can connect you with literature, podcasts, magazines, books, and other tools that will broaden your awareness. Once your resources are accessed, what should you do with them to inform your professional development? First things first, get inspired. While sorting through your newfound resources, highlight the points that resonate with you and your school's needs. Annotate articles and books. Screenshot the tweets of your favorite activists and educators. Dig deeper into this knowledge by further exploring terms, events, historical occurrences, and anything else these resources bring to light. Then prioritize. Make a list of three to seven important points you'd like to explore with faculty.

The creation and implementation of education policy is of great interest to Ms. Carroll, a middle-school counselor in Easton, Pennsylvania. She recently noticed a tweet from "Education Nation" highlighting transcending the classroom using civic engagement strategies. Her school had never hosted a professional development about civic engagement and no policies within the school specifically addressed civic engagement. Ms. Carroll wanted to get input from all faculty on what should be in place so that students felt heard. Ms. Carroll was aware of the racial dynamics at play, her school was predominantly black, and the staff was predominantly white. She leaned on the book by Chris Emdin, *For White Folks Who Teach In The Hood* (2017), to help inform her language and approach to this topic. She even made copies of excerpts from the book to use during the professional development activity. The activity itself included prior reading of the excerpts. Together with the whole group, Ms. Carroll made a list on the board of benefits and concerns. Together, the faculty discussed civic engagement as an issue of school-wide culture. The vice principal then gave six small groups of educators the current policy related to leaving school or school disruption. Each small group had to figure out a way to rewrite the policy. They made sure to also address the benefits and concerns on the board.

In developing professional development for your school, it is key to figure out the culture of your school and administration to know where you might best lead. Again, having some solutions to the questions you pose is often a great start to get investment from faculty. "I have some ideas to help address students frustration about the election" is a much better statement than "Students are frustrated about the election and we need to do something!" Below are seven alternative professional development ideas:

- Play a game of "Forehead" where you create the names of celebrities (making sure it is a diverse and inclusive group of options) on note cards for small groups to guess without viewing the card. The first group to correctly name ten people wins. Then lead a conversation about identity and the many words we use to describe difference.
- Watch a film, such as the documentary "Teach Us All," available on Netflix, and share thoughts related to race and identity after the movie.
- Watch a newscast of students participating in the behavior you would like to see at your school and brainstorm ways to encourage that behavior.
- Meme or cartoon analysis. Take social media memes, print them, and ask colleagues to analyze the themes as well as their use.
- Build the ideal school/program visual.
- Guest speaker.
- Name that student. Share positive aspects of a child's life and have colleagues guess which student you describe. For example, "she has curly brown hair, loves french fries, and always wears rainbow shoelaces".

These are a few of the litany of examples of professional development experiences you can facilitate in your building. Because teacher, counselor, and administrator responsibilities overlap, rely on innovation and creativity to be your guide. Lesson plans for students in Chapter 5 can even be adapted to fit a group of adult professionals. Don't reinvent the wheel, Teaching Tolerance (www.tolerance.org) is a great resource for classroom guidance lesson plans and teacher lesson plans.

As we think about social change on a societal, federal, state, local, and school-wide level, we have to remember to be the change we wish to see in our community. This work can feel overwhelming. Writing a letter to your state officials may feel daunting. Requesting a meeting with your principal and the superintendent may seem impossible. Our work calls on us to positively affect the lives of our students. Some of our students are suffering. Other students are craving the necessary skills, such as empathy and compassion, to end suffering in their peers. We must act and continue to act until all of our students are reaching their full potential.

Student–Counselor System Level

Our time with students is sacred. Our ability to reflect on our work with them will lead to best practice. The outcome of students' time with us will demonstrate the impact we have had on their lives. Identifying our biases, shifting our focus, and noticing our shortcomings are ways in which we can insure students are receiving the best we have to give. ASCA encourages collecting, analyzing, and interpreting data because numbers confirm much of what we believe to be true. Sometimes, data can show us what we have overlooked. When thinking about student-level reflections, let's examine three key areas: access to achievement, counselor contact, and engagement.

Access to achievement includes honors classes, gifted and talented programs, special education, graduation rates, Advanced Placement courses, International Baccalaureate programs, National Honor Society, and so much more. Are your students of color accessing opportunities to achieve? If you are a counselor in an all-white school, do your students understand why they attend a school with no (or few) racial differences? Do they believe this stifles or enriches their achievement? Why? As you begin or continue to collect data to disaggregate for race, keep accurate records of your findings and report your findings during leadership meetings. Be innovative, creative, and inclusive with your solutions. Remember, students are not responsible for educating you about their lived experiences, but they should be included in creating solutions. Do your homework but invite the student voice. Lastly, analyze the process by which students are selected for programs.

Record who comes to your office and when. This data may give you a window into how approachable you are to students as well as how inviting your space may be. Remember, biases inform your behavior. As counselors we do not choose which students are in our building. Is there a pattern to which students come to you? Look around your office, is it accessible to all types of students and physical body types? Where in the school is your office located? Which classrooms do you frequent? How do you seek out students who have not come to you? Feedback is important. Ask your student what it's like coming to visit the counselor's office. When I began working at a multi-diverse high school in downtown DC, my students would share an ominous "ooooooooooh" each time

I pulled a student. The suggestion was that the student was in trouble because they were being seen by the counselor. I realized that I had to change that perception of my role within the school.

Engagement centers around every other aspect of school climate, culture, and life. Are students participating and involved in school-wide activities in and out of the classroom? Are students happy to be in school? Attendance trends can show a story about engagement, particularly as it relates to race and socio-economic status. Do students feel welcome in school? School counselors can research tools that will aid in determining not only if students are engaged, but if all different types of students are engaged. Engagement is known to have a lasting impact on how well students perform.

When we do not professionally reflect in order to change systems that do not work for students of color, we are complicit in normalizing racism for all students and all faculty. We are indirectly and directly communicating to students and their families that we will not attend to issues related to race and that race-related issues are not a value to the school leadership. Many administrators and educators may not believe racism is a problem. Chances are, you believe racism is a problem or you are at least willing to determine if racism is a problem at your school. Your belief doesn't necessarily mean that your school leadership agrees. The hope lies in the fact that you are working your way through the details of these activities and you are better understanding the system in which you work. By understanding that system, you can best confront that system. In Chapter 8, we will introduce examples to help you form the language and ideas related to tackling this work.

Points to Consider

- Involvement in local government is a great way to understand how legislation affects your school.
- Having a general sense of how the Department of Education operates could impact and inform your level of activism and advocacy.
- Federal and state decisions will impact your school in some way. It's best practice to learn how your school will be impacted.
- As a school leader, you can influence the policies in your school with data evidence and a social justice lens.
- Engagement, attendance, and participation trends are telling. Analyze the data with respect to race.
- Your students need you to do this work.

References

Baltimore Sun. (2018, January 3). Letter: Baltimore City teachers union asks to close schools amid cold spell. *Baltimore Sun*. Retrieved from www.baltimoresun.com/news/maryland/baltimore-city/bs-md-cold-schools-20180103-story.html.

Caucus of Working Educators. (2018, June 3). *Join the caucus and TAG for the 5th annual summer reading series*. Retrieved from www.workingeducators.org/5th_annual_summer_reading_series.

Cox, D., Navarro-Rivera, J., & Jones, R. P. (2016). *Race, religion, and political affiliation of Americans' core social networks*. Public Religion Research Institute.

Emdin, C. (2017). *For white folks who teach in the hood ... and the rest of y'all too: Reality pedagogy and urban education*. Boston, MA: Beacon Press.

Howard, J. (2016, October 14). Students of all races favor teacher diversity, and here's why. *CNN*. Retrieved from www.cnn.com/2016/10/14/health/teacher-diversity-student-preferences/index.html.

Hughes, R. L. (2014, May 29). 10 signs of institutionalized racism. *Diverse Issues in Higher Education*. Retrieved from https://diverseeducation.com/article/64583.

Mazzola, J. (2017, March 20). Elementary students hold mock slave auction during class. *NJ Advance Media*.

National Education Association. (2016). *Discipline and the school-to-prison pipeline: 2018 NEA national meeting*. Retrieved from https://ra.nea.org/business-item/2016-pol-e01-2.

Office of the State Superintendent of Education, DC (2018). *DC Tuition assistance grant*. Retrieved from https://osse.dc.gov/dctag.

U.S. Department of Education, National Center for Education Statistics. (2018, May). *Public high school graduation rates* [Condition of Education national report].

Willingham, A. (2018, April 17). 'Who is Meek Mill and why do we want to free him?' Someone, somewhere, is in dire need of this article. *CNN*. Retrieved from https://edition.cnn.com/2018/04/13/entertainment/free-meek-mill-incarceration-rapper-trnd/index.html

Part III

Building Capacity of Stakeholders

Chapter 7

Stories from the Field

Real World Application of Equity in School Counseling

Imagine a school where equity is a topic that is frequently a part of open, trusting conversation. Where all stakeholders recognize that problems that exist outside of the school walls also exist within. The ideas shared in Chapters 4–6 explore self-reflection activities for self, students, and staff. The change that will ultimately happen at your school will begin when all stakeholders actively work together.

Where best to start than with school counselors who are working for equity? In this chapter, we will meet school counselors from all over the country who have implemented different strategies to move their schools toward an equitable education for all and discuss practical ideas for implementing in your school.

Andrew J. Knoblich
Career Development Coordinator
Charlotte-Mecklenburg Schools

Clare Merlin-Knoblich
Assistant Professor
University of North Carolina at Charlotte

We created and implemented an intervention known as *Diversity Dinner Dialogues*. In these dialogues, combinations of students, faculty members, and staff members from K-12 schools and a university College of Education faculty member read a selected diversity-related book, then come together over dinner to dialogue about the book, their school, and social justice in their community. In Fall 2016, we implemented one Diversity Dinner Dialogue at a local elementary school, bringing together faculty and staff members at that school with faculty and staff members at the University of North Carolina at Charlotte College of Education. Participants read a book about using culturally responsive practices in K-12 schools. In Spring 2017, we implemented two Diversity Dinner Dialogues at a local high school, where faculty and staff members joined high-school students to dialogue about a book highlighting the racial, socioeconomic, and cultural differences among specific individuals.

None of our three dinner dialogues would have been possible without funding. We were fortunate to get a small university grant for the first dialogue, plus a larger community grant for the second and third dialogues. These grants allowed us to purchase books, meals, and participant incentives. Collaboration with school leadership was also essential to gain approval for the programs. After communicating the intentions and possible outcomes of the program to key stakeholders, we were able to secure appropriate access to facilities and support that were necessary to make the program a success.

In all three dinner dialogues, we collected formal quantitative data before and after the events to examine if participants' multicultural attitudes had changed. Findings showed that participants' multicultural attitudes were, in fact, more positive several months after the dialogue than before. This data is exciting. Although it is tentative, given small sample sizes and a new intervention, it suggests that Diversity Dinner Dialogues may be useful tools to teach students and educators about multicultural differences and enhance their attitudes towards others who are different than themselves.

Anecdotally, we're most proud of the positive feedback we received about the dialogues. In particular, the appreciation from students of color, a small minority in the high school, stands out. For example, an Assistant Principal shared with us that when the Diversity Dinner Dialogues were announced at the school, several black students reached out to her with excitement. They expressed their appreciation for an event acknowledging race and multicultural differences. One student mentioned that even though she was not able to participate due to scheduling, the dinner dialogue made her feel seen and heard as a Black student at the school. The feedback was a reminder that so often students of color, or those in other minority groups, do not feel like their identities are acknowledged. It was a small hint that perhaps Diversity Dinner Dialogues are one step in an effort to counter that experience.

Our next step is to think even bigger. At the end of each dinner dialogue, participants commented, "what's next?" The dialogues seemed to catalyze a movement of energy and passion for social justice that we did not have continued funding or plans to nurture. In the future, we may create an extended series of multicultural awareness programming to create sustainable change and make a larger impact on schools, students, educators, and communities.

Lessons Learned

Gather support for your equity work by incorporating community building and fellowship. The visibility of your work for equity is important.

Miles Catlett
School Counselor
Davie County Early College High School, Mocksville, NC

I discovered the program Show Racism the Red Card and wrote a grant to visit the UK where the program is implemented. Upon returning, I taught many of the lessons in the classroom, mostly at the ninth grade level. This curriculum deals with stereotypes, differences, the media, and racism. It has literacy and technology components as well. I have also addressed racism in the school in different ways, like leading a short, whole-school session on the 'N' word or talking to small groups of students about racism.

The biggest obstacle I have faced is myself. I was initially afraid to address these topics with my students. I spent a lot of time reading, listening to podcasts, and traveling in order to gather the courage to do something. In a rural NC county where racism and bigotry are still very visible, and where whites are in the majority, it can be a little scary to begin talking about racism. You feel like you are stepping out on a limb, and you wonder what the response will be. You also worry about how different students respond. Will students of color feel singled out or uncomfortable? It has been important for me to learn as much as I can so I don't inadvertently do anything that harms a student.

I'm proud of my students and the culture of our school. Students are very tolerant and accepting of each other. When racism does occur, it's very swiftly dealt with; it doesn't linger because students won't stand for it. I'm always trying to find more ways for students to connect to each other's stories. I continue to search for ways for students to be able to share their stories with each other, while still helping students feel comfortable and allowing them to retain their privacy when they need to.

Lessons Learned

Use curriculum that has been successfully implemented as a starting place. Don't allow your own fears of failure impede this important work. Empower your students to embrace equity as part of the climate of the school.

Lauren Jones Austin
Career and Technical Education Program Director
Colorado Community College System, Denver, Colorado

I inquired from a handful of counselors statewide. In Colorado as a state, many of our schools are working very hard in ensuring equal access to AP/IB and higher-level classes through recruitment and individual student coaching. Some schools are recruiting bilingual counselors to assist families in their home languages about college opportunities and conducting student and parent workshops in their home languages.

Lessons Learned

Challenge the status quo of the systems and processes in your district.

Tanya Ilela
School Counselor
Hinkley High School, Aurora, Colorado

We have started two organizations at the school: African American Male Empowerment and Success (AAMES) and sponsored the development of Strong African American Female Empowerment (SAAFE). The male program has a student leadership team and focuses on positive navigation of the educational system (systemic oppression) through Voice and Choice, Critical Consciousness, Mentoring (representation matters), and Active Learning. We have an annual AAMES summit that brings our students and African American men from the community together, plus multiple other events throughout the year. Additionally, our student leadership team is mentoring African American male students at our feeder middle school. You can learn more on our website www.aamesuccess.org.

Lessons Learned

Empower students to be the change that is needed in your school. Incorporate feeder schools and community organizations to expand your impact.

Logan Laszczyk
School Counselor
Colorado Springs, Colorado

A team of administrators, teachers, counselors, and support staff made a conscious effort to open up AP classes to students, invite them to participate, encourage students, and express to parents/guardians our confidence in their child's ability to be successful in advanced coursework. The number of AP participants went up overall with an increase of females in math AP classes and an overall large increase of our black and Hispanic student population. We set a goal, we laid out high expectations for students, we expressed confidence, we checked-in often, and we encouraged the students to go for it.

We have held Friday forums where students, teachers, counselors, and administrators come together and talk about concerning issues. Some of these issues include divisions among race. Because the group is led by a school counselor and has students of various races, backgrounds, and interests (academics, athletics, musical performance, etc), the goal of the group is to have discussions on which the school can improve. No topic is off-limits.

Lessons Learned

Use data to identify students who might be underserved in your school and implement a plan to address this inequity. Listen to the voice of all students.

Central Office Administrators
Denver Public Schools, Denver, Colorado

In our current roles, we are addressing issues of racism from the perspective of developing equity and interrupting racism both within us as individuals, within our department, and without, through our interactions with school teams and students. We've seen people have ceremonies where they "buried the N-word," conducted student panels, had poetry slams and art/photo exhibits. Students have presented at our district-level Equity Boot Camps and talked to staff about their experiences. One school did a year-long study of a comparison of historical and contemporary practices and how they impacted society. Students were encouraged to explore how they would change the decisions that were made.

What we would like to see is for schools to bring in current news and issues within the schools to morning meetings on a daily basis, and to teach teachers and students how to have difficult conversations when they are needed. I have seen counselors respond to micro-aggressions or racially insensitive comments with the phrase: "What do you mean by that?"

Lessons Learned

Take on the work of equity with all stakeholders. Embed equity conversations in curriculum when possible.

Daniel Sandoval
College and Career Success Coordinator
Aurora Public Schools Division of Equity in Learning, Aurora, Colorado

At our school, Castle View High School, we celebrate a Diversity Week. This week is filled with activities, speakers, break-out sessions, and content in classrooms. We also use Restorative Practices, when appropriate, in working with students in individual settings when racism has occurred.

Lessons Learned

Highlight diversity in a special occasion and then continue to support through effective daily practices.

Liz Herlinger
School Counselor
J.C. Parks Elementary School, Indian Hand, Maryland

Students at our middle school were not understanding their actions and how they were affecting other students. We were concerned that bullying would increase so the counseling team decided to implement "The Ripple Effect" lessons. We made a PowerPoint presentation about the meaning of the ripple effect. In short, we explored how actions cause certain reactions and/or consequences to occur. We watched a YouTube video called "Respect: Start the Ripple." We asked students to sign a contract as a part of a Positive Ripple Effect. It stated: "With my words and actions, I pledge to be respectful, responsible, safe, and proud. I will allow my words and actions to cause a respectful, responsible, safe, and proud positive ripple effect on our school." Finally, we showed the students a music video called *Never Ever* by Keenan West.

We faced obstacles along the way. Some of the students did not take this seriously and thought this whole thing was a waste of their time and a joke. When the kids did not take the presentation seriously by either talking, laughing, playing, or sleeping, the other counselor and I called it out immediately and we addressed it. We made sure that the students understood that their behavior was the reason that we were doing the presentation.

A lot of students did take this campaign very seriously, so they took the initiative to make sure that other students were making the right choices in tough situations. Our eighth graders really became the leaders of the Ripple Effect movement in our school. They tried to set good examples for others. When I or the other counselor talked with students, it was nice to refer back to the presentation. If we were to do it again, we would expand the lesson to include engaging activities.

Lessons Learned

Don't assume that your students have the skills needed to show the equitable behaviors you are seeking. Teaching students the skills needed to respect each other may be an important step.

Tylon Crook, PhD, NCC
Core Faculty
Walden University School of Counseling, Minneapolis, Minnesota

Over the past two school years, I have focused my equity work at the school level on two areas that were identified by disaggregating data at my school. African American female students were under-represented in higher-level mathematics and science courses. Many of the African American students who attend our public residential School for Mathematics and Science come from traditional schools that either underprepare or do not push/encourage this population to take higher-order math and science courses. Only about 2 percent graduate having taken advanced courses in math and science. Our state has about a 38 percent African American population. The public school population is 50 percent African American with this population being split almost in half between boys and girls. Our School for Mathematics and Science currently has a 22 percent African American population, with the African American male population comprising only 5 percent of our overall school population.

Our department created a program to identify and funnel our targeted population into higher order math and science courses. This included: (1) intentional and focused career and college counseling and planning with students; (2) collaborating with teachers; (3) open and transparent conversations with parents; (4) sponsoring or conducting career days and connecting students with mentors in targeted careers that require higher-order math and science courses. In order to do so, we made the time to review and analyze data. My school counseling department schedules one hour per week to do nothing but analyze data. We worked to build and maintain a collaborative working relationship with school administration, making sure to communicate how our efforts benefit all students and the entire school.

The largest obstacle faced was the issue of African American students not having the opportunity to complete prerequisite courses that would allow them to take higher-order math and science courses. Because many students come from schools where the prerequisite courses are not even offered, it is difficult to catch them up within the two years that they spend at our school.

We also faced the obstacle of getting buy-in from the entire school staff. Because this is an institutional issue, it is imperative that all must be aware of and make concerted efforts to address it. It was difficult getting buy-in even though data was shared in a very comprehensive and descriptive manner with administrative approval.

The results that I have been most proud of include raising both issues enough that they are now on the priority list of the entire administrative staff and most of the school staff. I am also proud that I have been charged with building and leading a task force to address both issues. Finally I am proud of the ever so small gains that have been made through the efforts of the school counseling department, as we have made a concerted effort to implement a program that identifies and funnels more African American girls into higher-order mathematics and science courses.

If I were to begin these efforts again, the only thing I would change would be my approach. In addressing equity work it is important to be politically savvy in communicating with all stakeholders. Many were reluctant to receive and act on the information that was provided, even with administrative support. As every school is different, future options will include collaborating with administration to take a more directive approach.

Lessons Learned

Work to break down barriers to equity takes purposeful planning, collaborating, and enrolling all stakeholders in order to be effective.

Lauren Brand
School Counselor
Sycamore Creek Elementary School, Raleigh, NC

At the school level, our Instructional Leadership/School Improvement team saw discrepancies in our data and noticed that we, like many other schools, have pretty large opportunity gaps. Our school is very fortunate to be well resourced in many areas, so this really puzzled me. Tackling inequities is a TEAM EFFORT. We must communicate why it is important and engage key people in your school that will listen, collaborate, and spark a change. For me, this was our school's admin, Instructional Resource Teacher, school psychologist, and some teachers.

We dug deeper to find the foundational skill we needed to build. It became clear that we had to look at the relationships we had and our response to families that lived farthest from our school. These families are more likely to be lower socioeconomic status and may also have difficulty traveling to our school.

We coordinated a Thanksgiving Community Outreach using a grant that we received. Instead of the expectation of these families coming to us, we entered their community. I called each one of the 200 families that lived farthest away from the school to ask if they wanted a Thanksgiving meal on us. Of those who responded, we borrowed buses from surrounding middle and high schools, broke up into teams, and then delivered the meals the day before break. It was a ton of work, but an absolute blast. The children and teachers loved having extra time together to visit and some teachers were able to meet and engage with families that might otherwise not have been able to come to school.

From there, education was the next step. I knew we couldn't expect change without showing the staff and faculty our data and working through concrete action steps. With help from our district administration (and co-author of this book, Rebecca Atkins) and many personal educator friends, I developed an equity professional development that went over our school specific data, included information of what equity is, and then gave beginning action steps. The feedback I received is so enlightening as to where we can go from here. Currently, lessons are being developed, book lists are being shared, communication devices are being looked into, and so much more is going to happen. I am excited to continue the education and hone in on more specific goals to slowly begin the eradication of achievement gaps at our school.

We are a large elementary school which means that the staff are at various degrees of understanding of equity and buy-in to changing structures that have always been in place. Therefore, I had to start at the most foundational aspect: building a relationship. As I was planning the professional development, I received the most wonderful piece of advice from an educator friend who has started an equity PLT at her school: If you try to work on the people least accepting of change first, you will burn out. Start where you see the light bulb going on. Bring them in and celebrate the work they've started. Then, as the change begins to happen, reach out and lift the others. It will happen. Her advice really grounds me and helps me on the days where I am most frustrated with the process and the systematic pushback that naturally happens when you bring up hard conversations. I am still learning and growing myself, so I do not always have all the answers. Taking time for self-reflection and then signing up for professional development on my own time has helped me. Do not be afraid to reach out and collaborate with those around you.

It's hard to pinpoint what I am most proud of because there is so much left to do. I could say that I am most proud of our school and the willingness of educators and administration to have those critical conversations and look deeply at themselves and the school environment. I am most proud that it is on everyone's radar, and we are improving every day. In retrospect, I would have developed a better system of tracking all this change. I feel like the pieces are all around our school: in my office, classrooms, emails, etc., and it is not always conducive to my organized mind. So, in the future, when I have a bit more time, I am going to organize where we have been, where we are, and what we have left to do in our fight for equity in our school.

Lessons Learned

Start where you are with a team. Work first with those who are invested and wait for the change to spread before breaking down the most difficult barriers.

Kinea Epps
Lead School Counselor
Rolesville Middle School (RMS), Rolesville, NC

Our work began by examining our personal beliefs at the onset of our school-wide training on the Multi-Tiered System of Support (MTSS) and by exploring equity and access for all. We explored as a staff how our own experiences relate to equity in our school. In one Professional Development activity, each staff member engaged in the "How Diverse is Your Universe?" activity, where staff were asked to put beads in the cup to answer questions about where in your space in life is there diversity? For example, have you ever had dinner with someone of a different race? What is the racial makeup of your neighborhood? Outside of school, how diverse is your life? Compare and contrast to the break-down of your classroom.

As conversations and training continued within the school, our principal was formally trained as part of a district-wide effort and completed the Courageous Conversations training and applied that learning as the staff continued our equity work. Three of our teachers applied and were accepted to Project Ready (Reimagining Equity and Access for Diverse Youth) and then facilitated a staff book study on *Why Are All the Black Kids Sitting Together in the Cafeteria?*. The book club was optional and met once a month. We engaged in a Socratic-seminar to discuss our learning and to share our learning. One of the activities we did was to have each participant write down one quote that resonated with them from the book. We mixed them up and passed the cards around to read aloud anonymously.

Simultaneously, my principal and I attended the Courageous Conversation Summit in Detroit. We furthered our CC group with our staff. One grounding question we discussed as a staff was: "Where do we need to review our practices?" From this group, we formed the RMS Equity Team. In this team, we focus on cultural diversity, staffing decisions, and discipline policies and procedures.

Our school uses our professional development time during early release days for reviewing school-wide data and focusing on equity (examining classroom instruction, PBIS structures, intervention, and enrichment). We are planning an equity summit with other middle schools. Each school will send 20 students and we will have break-out sessions and guest speakers. The students who participate will then be prepared to be leaders in their own buildings. One of our next steps is to include racial disaggregation in more of our data analysis. For instance, not just negative behavior referrals but how many kids of color are recommended for Character Ed and positive phone calls.

Lessons Learned

Intentionality leads to success. Use opportunities that are available to you to enrich and enhance the work of equity.

Conclusion

The best outcomes come from strategies and ideas that meet the needs of the school. Consider the strengths and weaknesses of your school; highlight three activities from these real-world examples and the reflection activities that we shared in Part 2 that you would like to implement. Consider the following for each:

- What factors within your school and community will increase the likelihood of success?
- What factors within your school and community will decrease the likelihood of success?
- Who can you tap as an ally in making your idea into a plan of action?
- What resources will you need? Who can provide these resources?

Once you have a plan, create a timeline of when you plan to implement. Change won't happen until you begin.

Chapter 8

Interrupting Racism
Everyday Scenarios

Working in a school environment can be joyful, engaging, and almost always spontaneous. As practitioners are well aware, lived experiences with staff, students, and communities can catch you off guard and challenge your expertise. Think critically about the role of each individual, the history of each individual, and the goals of education and school counseling and let these roles influence your perspective when interrupting racism. We want the responses cultivated to be informed and reflective so that you can continue to grow into the kind of school counselor and leader your students need. Additionally, as society shifts, our students' needs shift, we will explore the implications of each scenario through a social justice lens and the roles of the school counselor as advocate, leader, and collaborator for systemic change. As you explore each scenario in this chapter, be sure to notice themes, write your thoughts, and post in your office reminders of your baseline philosophy. This is to help ground you and center you during what is normally a very busy, time-consuming and habit-inducing school year.

Scenario One

During a classroom lesson, the school counselor is teaching about the concept of persistence in a time of controversy. The school counselor uses the example of Jackie Robinson being the first black baseball player in the entirely white major league. The school counselor reads the story "Stealing Home: The Story of Jackie Robinson" by Barry Denenberg. She asks the class questions about how Jackie Robinson was treated and what he did to overcome being mistreated. A student in class responds: "All white people are racist. That's what my mom said!" The teacher doesn't respond, waiting for the school counselor to interject. The class laughs at the child's comment and you have not directly covered the topic of racism in your lessons as of yet.

As the counselor, you have indirectly introduced this concept of racism as a topic for discussion in class. By no means does that mean this is the first time students have been introduced to the word, its meaning, or its misuse. The student feels comfortable enough in class, and with everyone in the room, to voice their thoughts. This is a huge positive. We want students to be able to share anything and everything that is on their mind so that we can help guide them. It's difficult to steer, mold, influence, and prepare students for life when we don't know their perspectives, beliefs, and opinions. We want to be sure to offer positive reinforcement to the students in this situation even if their comment is controversial, after all, our very topic for this lesson is persistence during controversy.

We are living the moment we are teaching but instruction is the most effective when we know our end goal or learning objective. The second idea is that we must know, in advance, what our end goal is. We must know what we want students to leave our lesson with and how to frame our responses, and their learning, so that students learn the message we intend to teach. The message may not be that "all white people were mean to Jackie Robinson" but instead the lesson's takeaway might be "how to examine how others are treated." With this in mind, the comment becomes less the focus of the story and more a tangent to the bigger picture. Third, consider the demographics of the school. The dynamics are different with a racially homogeneous population. Reflect on how this comment might be shared and received amongst a racially diverse group.

Reflection

Ask yourself the following questions to process this scenario:

- In a racially homogeneous school, how might the demographics affect how the students comment is approached?
- In what ways does the student's comment confirm or negate the overall message of the classroom guidance lesson about Jackie Robinson? In other words, how is it relevant or irrelevant, helpful or unhelpful to the overall message of persistence during controversial events?
- How can you transform the student's comment to be helpful if it is not?
- In what developmentally appropriate ways can you adapt your lesson if it does not already include an opportunity for students to share their beliefs about race and racism?
- What is your reaction to blanket statements such as the one the student made? What life events and experiences have helped to shape your reaction?

The school counselor responds by saying:

> What you shared, Dyshon, is really thought-provoking. Does everyone know what thought-provoking means? Yes/Almost, it means to make someone pause and think. It's tough to know what all people are like because there are millions of people in the world. But what we can learn from Jackie Robinson's story is that when someone doesn't like you or value you, there are ways in which you can tell. How can you tell some of these people did not value Jackie Robinson, what did they do?

This response allows for multiple opportunities. The first opportunity is for the school counselor to show calm in the face of controversy, the very theme they are teaching for the lesson. The second opportunity is to introduce the idea of microaggressions in developmentally appropriate language while maintaining the primary goal: How to examine how others are treated. The response lends itself perfectly to that accord.

The school counselor is feeling especially bold and confident about her knowledge, so she says:

> What you shared, Dyshon, is really impactful. Who in this class agrees with Dyshon? Tell me why you agree … (some responses or no responses are shared). Ok, so I want to be sure we are all on the same page. All white people are not racist in the ways Jackie Robinson tells his story. There are white people who value black people and want us to be safe and equal and valued. Would you like me to share some examples of who those people are?

This response allows for two identified opportunities. The first opportunity is for the school counselor to correct misinformation. She can share examples of people and how their lives are committed to anti-racism. She assumed the position of an expert within the school on race related issues. The second opportunity is to validate the students need to be safe, equal, and valued. Dyshon's mom may have expressed this statement out of fear for the safety of her family. Racism in its ugliest forms is a danger. Blanket statements in all communities are often expressed out of fear of the unknown. Without vilifying Dyshon and/or his mother, we can understand why statements like this are sometimes made, and reframe the statements.

Scenario Two

After nationwide protests to end gun violence, a small group of students at McAsca High School want to organize and plan their own protest during the school day. The administration denies their request to protest during school hours but gives the students the option to plan a small protest after school hours and with parent permission. The small group of students is racially and economically diverse. The group assumes the title "A Silent Few" and plans a peaceful protest that will spend five minutes in total silence outside of school with banners and signs. On the day of the protest, students come to school with t-shirts with their group name and the names of students killed by gun violence in their community on the back. The administration calls two of the group members into the main office. The two students are told the protest is cancelled and they will serve detention for disruptive behavior. The students are stunned and caught off guard because they have no idea how they were being disruptive. The students leave the office and tell everyone else in the group that the protest is cancelled. The remaining group members are furious and refuse to officially cancel the protest. They tell everyone in school to attend and bring their signs. At the end of the school day, the students continue their protest as planned. The protest is successful with over 100 students and faculty members participating. The two students serve their detention and attend the protest as it concludes. The next day, the same two students who served a detention are again called into the office. They are notified that they will be suspended due to their refusal to cancel the protest. The two students are black and identified as the leaders of "A Silent Few."

Reflection, Part I

As the school counselor, you have been made aware of the events as they occur. Reflect on the following questions identifying themes you find important to address and include in your response/interruption:

- What are the demographics of the student body? What are the demographics of the school leadership?
- Who made the disciplinary decision and why was this the decision made? Did you know about the decision and did you have input?
- What is the data on discipline at this high school disaggregated for race? Are either of these students identifying with any other marginalized group? Disaggregate for those identities as well (special education, LGBTQ, etc.).
- Is the process for disciplinary action the same for all students? How do we know?
- What are the political views of the surrounding community? What is the political climate of the surrounding community? Are these students' political views within the minority at school and/or in the surrounding community?
- How would you have wanted to see this situation handled? What would you have wanted the students to learn from their desire to be activists? How does your history with activism influence this?

Student activism has long been a part of our society. Laws are in place to protect students' rights and, as school counselors, we must be aware of these rights and ready to protect student rights within our school buildings. Yet schools are continuously denying students' rights to protest in peaceful ways. Here are a few suggestions of how school counselors can respond should an event similar to this happen within their school.

Know the Law and Give Care

The American Civil Liberties Union (ACLU) has shared information about protecting students' rights to protest on their blog:

> Since the law in virtually all jurisdictions requires students to go to school, schools can typically discipline students for missing class, even if they're doing so to participate in a protest or otherwise express themselves. But what the school can't do is discipline students more harshly because they are walking out to express a political view or because school administrators don't support the views behind the protest. In other words, any disciplinary action for walking out cannot be a response to the content of the protest.
>
> (Eidelman, 2018, second para.)

Given this standard, the school counselor responds in a way that supports the students and acknowledges the school context, both the leadership and community perspectives. The counselor informs the principal that they plan to meet with the students to discuss the disciplinary action. During the meeting, the counselor offers encouragement of the student being expressive and wanting to organize a response to school violence. The counselor takes time to hear how the discipline has impacted the students and to validate the students' experience, and validates any harboring resentment while genuinely reassuring students that they are heard and understood. If students have questions about their rights, the counselor directs them to where they can find the information. Afterwards, the counselor debriefs with the principal to bridge between students and administration. School climate is improved when the two understand each other's position.

Identify Free Speech Versus Hate Speech

While we want our students to freely speak their minds, we want them to know that our beliefs, words, and actions have an impact on others. We teach some aspects of morality to kindergarteners (Be kind, use kind words, keep our hands to ourselves) and we will likely find similar messages in our work with older children. A simple distinction that can be made for students who struggle to differentiate free speech from hate speech is the impact the words have on others. Counselors asks the group of students: Who do your words affect? How does it affect them? Why do you want to affect other students/people in that way? These are key questions that can reveal the underlying objectives of a student's language and actions. All protests are not created equal and we can discover how various incidents of student activism can affect our school climate.

Reflection, Part 2

Explore the data and make a list of concerns. After reviewing the reflection questions and the scenario at your school, were any instances of racism revealed? If not, continue to support your student body and consider preventative ways of handling student activism in the future. If the data suggests that black students and/or marginalized students are being disciplined at a higher rate than white students, you have a bigger problem than just student protests. Prepare a summary or report of the data you have collected and share with your leadership team at the next meeting. Your language may be something close to this:

> Good morning, I wanted to take some time to review some of our practices. After the incident with "A Silent Few" I ran a few reports to make sure we were doing everything we were supposed to and discovered that some of our data is skewed. If you look at the top chart, you'll see our entire student body broken down by race and percentages. If you compare it to the bottom chart, you'll notice our kids with discipline referrals broken down by race and percentages. As you can see, these two charts are not the same, which means our practices are disproportionately and negatively impacting our black students.

Be prepared with solutions. Use inclusive language that makes you a part of the solution. Do not blame the disciplinary team, this will only lead to tension and conflict. The goal is to create a better school environment for students and a learning opportunity for staff.

Prevention should be a high priority. High schools are places where students are increasingly finding their voice. Be sure to build into your program opportunities for students to express themselves.

Scenario Three

A classroom of fifth graders is reading the 1960 book *Island of the Blue Dolphins* by Scott O'Dell about an indigenous family that faces evacuation of their home. The teacher introduces to the students several themes including historical fiction style reading/writing, cultural fluency, and gender stereotypes. The school counselor is asked to supplement the week's reading with additional conversation and activities about these themes. During a workshop with the fifth graders exploring cultural fluency, students are given the task to locate the distribution of indigenous tribes over 100 years on a map. A fifth grade student says: "This is stupid. Aren't all the Indians dead? Why do we have to read about them when they aren't even around anymore?" The teacher responds: "We have to do this because the new guidelines for class include learning about different cultures." As the school counselor, you are unsure of how to respond in the moment so you don't intervene.

Later that day, you are asked to join a brief meeting in the principal's office because the student's parents have called and would like their child to be exempt from the discussion and activities. As the school counselor, we are given opportunities throughout each day to interrupt. Occasionally, we miss an opportunity and you know that you missed a learning opportunity in this lesson.

Reflection

The students perspective is shared verbally in class. What might your initial visceral reaction be to such a statement? The student speaks from a position of authority as if they know this information they are sharing to be true. Is that common for this child? Does it matter what race this child belongs to? Why or why not? How did the other students respond to this comment? Are there indigenous children in this classroom? What might they need as a result of this incident?

The teacher's response to the student is a testament to what? Based on this teacher's response, how might you engage them in further debriefing of this incident? What supports if any can you offer the teacher right now? Is this an indication of a broader issue related to this teacher's cultural fluency and attitudes toward multiculturalism?

Your perspective, beliefs, history, and knowledge of indigenous people can be unpacked, reflected upon, and dissected with time and care. Refer back to Chapter 4 and your family tree. Think geographically. Where do you live? What is the larger community's relationship to indigenous people. Your answer may vary greatly if you live in New Mexico than if you live in Delaware. Take this into account to better understand your perspective without judgement.

Contemporary issues such as DACA and immigration laws greatly influence families and their views on indigenous people. Are you familiar with current events around immigration? How can you increase your knowledge? Since the students parents have called requesting their child be removed from the lesson, how might your school respond? How might you respond? Review policy with leadership and be led by your social justice framework.

With practice comes improvement.

Use the lines below to craft a response to the parents in this scenario:

_____

_____

_____

_____

_____

_____

_____

This is not about blame or shame, we are tasking students to become more inclusive so we must model that behavior even in the most difficult of situations.

Scenario Four

During an elementary school assembly, you share slides about this month's school-wide volunteer event at "Casa de Ayuda." Among your slides are pictures of the families who are helped by the volunteer event where your students will pack sandwiches and read books to younger children. The third and fourth grade students seem excited to participate. You ask the group if anyone has any questions. A third grade student raises their hand and asks why the slides only show black people when the event is for Latinos. Some of the other children laugh at the student's remarks. The teachers and administrators smile at you, encouraging your response.

Reflection

As the school counselor, you are routinely involved in moments that require you to be clever, knowledgeable, and responsive. The school is watching, the counselor is leading, the faculty is expecting an appropriate and immediate response, you are under a lot of pressure. This is precisely the reason we are engaging you in thoughtful reflection about interrupting racism. Children say the "darndest" things because they are looking to us to provide them with the information they need to be contributing citizens, to make the world a better place for everyone. Reflect on the following questions:

1. How does your racial and ethnic identity fit amongst the school body? How does your membership or non-membership influence your response?
2. What has been the historical context of your racial and ethnic identity in contrast to the school body? Is it a positive part of the community? At a historical power advantage (Do students' home countries have a history of conflict)? Evaluate that history and dynamic using your reflection from Chapter 4.

3.   What has your student body already learned about skin color and race? If nothing, comments such as this may be an indicator that students want to learn more. What do you already know about skin color and the many Spanish-speaking and/or Latino countries? Developmentally, how can you incorporate this lesson into the community service event?

With practice comes improvement. Use the lines below to craft a response to this scenario:

_____

_____

_____

_____

_____

_____

_____

This is an opportunity to teach children and model behavior. This scenario is challenging because you are required to self-regulate while under pressure and while providing accurate and relevant information.

Scenario Five

This month's professional development is on classroom management strategies and engaging families. The presenters are community organization members who were invited to hear about the struggles your school is having with some student behaviors and to help educators practice engaging families in their child's education. Typically at this school, many families are involved in ways that can feel supportive and occasionally taxing on faculty time. When the presenters asked educators about this occurrence a teacher, Ms. Murphy, shared the following situation:

> A family came in to ask me why I paired their son with another student. They said their son was advanced and being held back by the other student. They were really insistent that I re-pair their child even though I didn't think anything was wrong. The parents are on the PTA and help every year with the bake sale so I didn't want them to pull their support but I felt bad for the students. The other child is African-American so I am not sure if it's because of that. I think both boys are about the same academically so I didn't know what to do.

Several teachers nod in agreement that this is a hard situation. Another teacher chimed in by sharing: "I don't think it's a race thing, the parents just want what's best for their kid."

Reflection

As the school counselor, let's focus on the second teacher's comment in this scenario. Coded language is often used to express a sentiment that may be based in racism. Few people want to be identified as racist, despite their beliefs and/or behaviors. The truth is that regardless of whether or not words are perceived as racist, our beliefs fuel our actions and language. Our beliefs can be explored, and thankfully, shifted in ways that reflect a better understanding of difference. Another aspect of this scenario we can confront is assigning the authority to dictate what is and isn't disproportionately negative towards marginalized groups. Unless the second commenting teacher is the director of diversity and inclusion or their role is specifically to identify racist practices, their self-assignment as the authority on racism must be interrupted. Lastly, we can use data to examine what is happening in the classroom based on demographics and other identifiers that may be at a disadvantage (knowingly or unknowingly) because of school practices.

Let's address the first aspect: coded language. A news segment on CNN in 2015 sought to unveil the hidden meaning behind the word "thug" to describe black protesters in Baltimore. In an article exploring the language used to describe "these people," *Vox* journalist German Lopez added the idea that "The way these words play into stereotypes without outright mentioning them gives the user some leeway" (Lopez, 2016, sixth para.). Ian Haney-López, a professor at University of California at Berkeley who wrote *Dog Whistle Politics: How Coded Racial Appeals Have Reinvented Racism and Wrecked the Middle Class* (2015), focuses on the way in which people use language to express their racist beliefs without consequence. As we continue to think critically, we must remember that language matters. We would never call our students bad names because we know the way in which abusive and degrading language affects a child's self esteem and morale. We have to be equally as diligent when our words convey our beliefs. Take the statement: "I don't think it's a race thing, parents just want what's best for their kid." This statement implies that (1) the commenter is an authority on what is or is not race-based without relevant credentials, knowledge, and/or expertise and (2) the teacher who has raised the concern is unable to gauge a potentially race-related issue in their class. We will continue to examine the idea of coded language such as "best for the child" in scenario 8. Because this is a common and dangerous belief system to hold within a school, let's jump to responding in the moment and reflecting as a part of debrief.

A response from the school counselor might sound like some version of the following as it pertains to both implications of the problematic statement:

> We should remain open, as a majority white school, to the possibility that at any moment, we could have a race-related issue here. That being said, I appreciate your reflection on your student's experience in your classroom, Ms. Murphy. It's important for us to be tuned in to what our students experience in the classroom. We have a commitment to families and we want to honor their input while also remaining in service to all of our students. I want to examine this situation further with you and any other

teacher who has the same issue. Can our PD presenters share any tips on how to help families understand what including others who might be different means in our classes?

Another response could be as follows:

> Before we decide what kind of concern this is, I'd like to follow-up on this with some data collection. I am happy to check and double-check whether or not any of our practices are marginalizing students, Ms. Murphy. Can our PD presenters offer any tips on how to communicate to parents next steps with this in mind?

Now, let's address the second aspect of this scenario. Another layer to your possible response is deciding in this moment whether or not to help the second teacher understand that she is not an authority on racial issues within the school, unless of course this person is the director of diversity and inclusion, in which case you may have a bigger issue. By attempting to extinguish the possibility that what is happening could be race-related, they are indirectly contributing to marginalization itself which can be harmful to students. Without publicly accusing the second teacher of wrongdoing, make it clear how race needs to be approached within our school. Without clearly stating the school's stance on race, we are indirectly sending a message that race is not to be broached.

Rely on everyone's shared value and consider the following response:

> We all want students to be cared for, loved, and valued so it is important for us to make sure nothing is standing in the way of that. I trust our faculty and I want us to make sure we are doing all we can to protect students.

Are we in the position as school counselors to educate faculty on race-related issues? That's for you and your principal to decide. Professional development has a beautiful way of exposing additional topics that can be explored in the future. This scenario is a perfect example of that instance.

Lastly, how do we maintain our engagement with families through this work. Viewing our practice through a social justice lens may be encouraged by our colleagues but what about families, parents, and guardians? Will the student's family say "We don't want our white child learning with a black child?" Likely no, and many parents do not hold that sentiment. Due to faulty beliefs, families and community members make associations that are not generally true or helpful—in this case, that the black student is below grade level and the parent's own child is not. Our responsibility is to advocate on behalf of all students and provide equity where there is need. While families and parents will advocate for their children, we advocate for all children.

We suggest a number of strategies as listed in Table 8.1.

With practice, you will be able to identify coded language and help parents reframe their concerns to be more reflective of reality and not misconceptions. For example, the student in this scenario has parents willing to advocate for the most rigorous experience in class. That within itself is wonderful. So we might turn this into the following response:

Table 8.1 Strategies for engagement with families

Language	Newsletters, invitations, announcements, flyers, report card summaries, website, course description, event descriptions, etc. Every piece of correspondence from your school should include inclusive language about diversity.
Visuals	Pictures of students should be displayed throughout the school. Families should be able to regularly encounter some visual representation of the student body. Is your school homogeneous? Be sure to include visuals that illustrate explicitly about difference in ways that are meaningful and not tokenism.
Intention	Practice using the vocabulary of social justice counselors. When families begin to hear these words more frequently they are more likely to anticipate changes and events related to diversity within the school setting.
Curriculum	Incorporate social justice standards (Appendix B) in your curriculum and purposefully create opportunities for students to learn about history and current events that relate to race and privilege.

Mr. and Mrs. Bell, I appreciate you encouraging Bill to push himself academically. Derek, his partner, is actually one of the best students in class to help facilitate this. I know you don't know Derek very well but his parents gave me permission to reach out and share some information that might help you with this pairing. Derek's constant curiosity about kinetic energy has proven to be motivational to your son, Bill. I hope to work with both boys well into the winter as they are learning so much from each other.

Additionally, this can also be shared with the teacher who may have some faulty beliefs about race. Every person is influenced by their history, their family, their community, the larger society, and many of those influencers have faulty information. We can be the corrective voice in our school.

Who do we have entering our schools and providing professional development? Having knowledgeable and socially conscientious professional development teams who are prepared to respond to these comments is crucial. PD presenters should also be prepared to invite these discussions if educators do not divulge their thoughts as an opportunity to reframe and educate and to further give reason for continued data collection. An important question has been raised. Is this black student being treated unfairly? Context is key. We are highlighting race as a way to view many variables of why a student may be excluded. Is race a factor? Is either student receiving special education? Does either student have a behavior modification plan, an individualized education plan, a 504 plan? Does the family have a history with the student and/or the student's family? Is sexual orientation and/or expression a factor? When we include all relevant questions, the possibility of race being a factor seems less unlikely and less daunting because as we know, many factors can contribute to a family's request for intervention.

Scenario Six

A teacher submits a referral sheet to you. He would like you to speak with one of his students who is looking to join the step team for the Black History Month (BHM) show. Each year, the Black History Month show brings students, faculty, and families to the all-school assembly for a high-energy and well-choreographed cultural extravaganza. You are unsure of exactly why the student would need a counselor intervention but you check in with the teacher as soon as you can. After school, you walk to the area where students are gathered to practice for the BHM show. You see a student seated by herself while a small group of girls practices step moves amongst themselves. You ask the teacher if the student is free to come to your office and he agrees. When you arrive in your office, the student tells you that she doesn't feel allowed to participate in the step performance because she's not black. You make a few clarifying statements such as "Help me understand what happened." The student tells you that when she signed up for the show the teacher told her that step was traditionally for black girls and boys. She expressed feeling confused because she identifies as black, but instead of explaining her race, she started to cry. You email the teacher and ask to meet with him the next day.

Reflection

With practice comes improvement. Use the lines below to craft a response to the student first and then subsequently the teacher in this scenario. Keep in mind how your response may differ if the student is white and wants to join the step team:

_____

_____

_____

_____

_____

_____

_____

This is not about blame or shame; we must preserve our relationships with fellow educators and show compassion when needed. A supportive and encouraging conversation with the teacher might resolve the issue.

Scenario Seven

Students enter your counseling office frustrated and arguing amongst their group. They ask to speak with you about an incident that occurred during their fifth period pre-calculus class. You have 15 minutes before the last bell of the day rings. You planned to finish printing a few documents for other students but realize you can get this done the following morning without interruption to your schedule. You tell the students, about six of them, to come into your office and shut the door behind them. You ask them if they are safe. They say yes. You ask them if they are hurt or need an ambulance. They say no. You tell them that you'd like to hear the story from one person and then others can share their thoughts. The students elect Daysia to tell you what happened. Daysia proceeds to describe their pre-calc class led by Ms. Bancroft. Ms. Bancroft is known throughout the school as being a very strict mathematics teacher for the higher-level grades. Daysia says:

> We were in pre-calc in our groups. Some of us were talking but most of us were listening to the lesson. She wasn't lecturing but she was telling us how to finish our project but some people were already starting their project and didn't need more instruction. So then I overheard her say "Black Lives Matter, you have to make it matter." A bunch of other people heard it. I didn't know what to do so I just looked around to see who else heard her. I was confused, like, why would you say that? What do you even mean by us having to make it matter? Like, where did that even come from?

As the counselor, you recognize the perspectives of students can often be skewed so you are fortunate to have several students to add their input. More students add comments such as:

> I was shocked at first but then I realized that she does say sneak stuff on the low. (She makes comments that can be interpreted in many ways but seem malicious in nature.)

> She may not be racist but that comment was not for a white person to say.

> I didn't like her before this moment but I really don't like her now.

> What did that have to do with what we were doing, Ms. Counselor?

> A couple of students got right back with her asking her what she was talking about and she didn't respond. (A couple of students quickly responded in defense to her statement to which she had no response.)

Reflection

As a counselor, you work with and for students at your school. We cannot completely remove ourselves from the business of teacher and student relationships because those relationships affect learning. This is a complicated scenario where we must not only explore the relationship these students have with Ms. Bancroft, but we must also explore the effect Ms. Bancroft's beliefs have on the students as well as the schools response to problematic teacher perspectives.

- Why is this a problematic teacher perspective? What problematic perspectives have you held as a counselor that can be a connecting point for you and the teacher? Remember, we are learning and growing together and at different paces.
- What is the relationship between Ms. Bancroft and students, historically? Have there been concerns about this teacher prior to this incident? First and

foremost, is the teacher aware that students are upset? If so, does leadership also know? If yes, what has been the response? If no, who is responsible for working with teachers in your building?

- How do Ms. Bancroft's beliefs affect students? Remember, we can often become very defensive of our students, particularly when we do not have regular contact and interaction with teachers. The less you know someone the easier it is for you to dislike them. We cannot remain isolated from the teaching staff. We must continuously work in collaboration to strengthen our relationships. Balancing compassion with critique takes practice.

With practice comes improvement, use the lines below to craft a response to students and Ms. Bancroft in this scenario:

_____

_____

_____

_____

_____

_____

_____

Remember to keep blame and shame out of your response.

Scenario Eight

The local school board hosts a townhall meeting for parents about the new busing program to help integrate schools in the community. A few faculty members from your school agree to attend the townhall meeting with you and raise questions about supportive programming in place for the efforts. When you arrive at the townhall, the school board begins the meeting with general announcements. They describe a new system in which the bordering neighborhoods that are predominantly black and Latino have entered into an agreement to allow 10 percent of their student population to enroll in and be bused to the local 95 percent white school district. You observe as parents and community members erupt in discontent. Some of the comments shared include: "It's not about race but those children don't share the same values as our community" and "Our tax dollars should be spent on the people who live here not other people's children." The school board informs the attendees that they must abide by stipulations handed down from the Department of Education. The faculty members you arrived with are silent.

Reflection

As a school counselor, our role as advocates for students and the profession is paramount. When placed in situations where we are representing students' best interests, we have to preserve our role. The townhall is a public event where we may be called on to respond on behalf of the wellbeing of students. The first issue is the meaning of wellbeing. Undoubtedly, the parents angry about this shift in school demographics would say it is "in the interest of the children." Recall the history of integration in public schools. Remember the images of Ruby Bridges and the Central Nine students walking into the school building, surrounded by police to prevent these children from attacks by "concerned parents." The sentiments are similar though possibly not as physically violent.

The second issue includes our own beliefs about integration. The authors of this book would venture to presume many educators reading already believe in some level of social justice. Integration allows students to learn from each other. Learning because of and in spite of difference builds character and empathy. Critical thinking is also a great benefit of learning across difference as it encourages children to add nuance to their perceptions. If you have not always believed integration is beneficial to students, explore the origin of that belief.

Finally, the third issue is a testament to the support and philosophy of your school. Does your principal fully support and want to encourage integration efforts? Meetings to strengthen and examine your school's mission should be reoccurring. With new structures, policies, and programs, faculty can work in collaboration to identify the position your school is taking on political and policy issues. For example, at a local public school in Washington, DC, a program providing funding to graduating seniors was in danger of being cut. The local high schools decided to take a political stance and petition their policy makers and government officials. They made phone calls, wrote letters, and flooded social media outlets with their position to reinstate the funding. Schools made a conscious effort to support the program in danger of being removed.

Well Being

What is your school counselor philosophy? How does race fit in your philosophy? How might your philosophy impact students who do not identify the same as you? Essentially, this is an exploration of difference. Your philosophy has implications for all students even if that is not your intention. When you think of wellbeing and what is best for students, how do you connect this to your philosophy? For example, my philosophy as a high-school counselor is "every student regardless of circumstance should have access and support to make informed choices about their plans after high-school graduation." My philosophy then means that wellbeing for students includes having access, having support and being able to make choices for themselves.

- The townhall is about integration efforts. After reading the Chapter 1 and exploring your family's history, what do you believe about integration? Who benefits from integration? Who suffers from the effects of integration?
- What is your school's stance on integration efforts? Do they support it but do nothing to implement it? Do they publicly express one belief but privately another? Again, know your context so that you can prepare.

What is the first plan of action when you return to school the next day? Why is this your choice?:

_____

_____

_____

_____

_____

_____

Refer to the system reflections of Chapter 6 when incorporating political, federal, and local government implications.

Scenario Nine

The superintendent is issuing a new policy that requires a new bullying curriculum be assigned to every school counselor in every school across your district. Your materials have arrived and you settle into your office to read the guidelines that you must adapt to your student body. You notice several concerns: (1) None of the parent handouts are in Spanish and your student population is 25 percent Latino. (2) All of the images on the handouts and materials are white students and teachers. (3) None of the details in the curriculum include race-based bullying. You consider speaking with your principal about your concerns but hesitate as you are new and do not want to draw undue attention.

Reflection

Frequently school counselors evaluate the appropriateness of curricula for our student population. Anti-bullying efforts are heavily utilized throughout Pre-K-8 education. Teaching classroom lessons that increase kindness and healthy relationships amongst your students is a desirable program. With many anti-bullying programs, there are sub-types of bullying that may occur in any given school included in the lesson. Cyber-bullying is a very frequent sub-type. Racialized bullying is not as commonly discussed. Racialized bullying would be synonymous with a hate crime on a larger scale. Bullying is about a power dynamic. When a student experiences a pattern of ongoing targeted behavior because of their race, the response needs to be equally as targeted and specific. Reflect on these questions:

- Has your school leadership approached the topic of racialized bullying before? If so, what happened? If not, has racialized bullying been reported in your school?
- How might you try to identify racialized bullying? What questions would you need to ask?

- Is your relationship with the principal able to withstand this critique? Is your principal willing to hear your feedback?
- The website StopBullying.gov (2017, first para.) explains that

> Schools and communities that respect diversity can help protect children against bullying behavior. However, when children perceived as different are not in supportive environments, they may be at a higher risk of being bullied. When working with kids from different groups, there are specific things you can do to prevent and address bullying.

As a prevention measure, how can you gauge whether or not your school climate is a supportive environment of difference?

- What might you do if your leadership team does not give you support or permission to include racialized bullying protections within your school? Even if you are in a racially homogeneous population, comments and attitudes towards varying groups can be prevalent. Interrupting racism not only occurs when black students encounter white students, it occurs at any given opportunity where race is potentially the topic or issue.

With practice comes improvement, use the lines below to craft a response to this scenario:

_____

_____

_____

_____

_____

_____

_____

_____

Difficulty Changing

Change is hard. Students, families, and community need firm support when navigating the complexities of changing their beliefs, beliefs they may have maintained for decades. Many scenarios described above are taken directly from current events. A 2018 *Atlantic* article details a scene where

> packed at a school board meeting, white parents one after another spoke out about their fears of this new incoming student population—that they'd bring increased crime, violence and disease. And, some parents feared how the black students tests scores might threaten their own children's academic standing.
>
> (Cohen, 2018, fourth para.)

The article was focused on a specific type of interruption where colleges and universities invest their attention and recruiting efforts on high schools that value, demonstrate, and are committed to diversity and inclusion. This interruption directly counters the historic practice of college admissions counselors primarily targeting predominantly white affluent high schools for visits and college fairs. Reflection for this interruption means asking yourself two important questions:

- How far am I willing to go to interrupt the harmful status quo?
- What will this interruption cost me?

Points to Consider

- Each scenario can be adapted to fit your school environment. Change details of the circumstance and imagine your responses.
- Practice makes better. Practicing your responses can help you feel more confident and prepared to interrupt racism when it happens.
- Do not obsess over mistakes. Practice self-care habits. Remember you are a work in progress and mistakes are learning opportunities.
- Racism will inevitably surface. You will get many chances to improve.
- Remember, all of these scenarios are opportunities to reflect and practice. When your information is limited, seek the supports and collaboration of outside resources. There are organizations and agencies that specialize in this work. Rely on them for help.

References

Cohen, R. M. (2018, May 23). An unusual idea for fixing school segregation. The Atlantic. Retrieved from www.theatlantic.com/education/archive/2018/05/an-unusual-idea-for-fixing-school-segregation/560930/.

Eidelman, V. (2018, February 22). Can schools discipline students for protesting? *American Civil Liberties Union*.

Haney-López, I. (2015). *Dog whistle politics: How coded racial appeals have reinvented racism and wrecked the middle class*. New York, NY: Oxford University Press.

Lopez, G. (2016, February 1). The sneaky language today's politicians use to get away with racism and sexism. *Vox*. Retrieved from www.vox.com/2016/2/1/10889138/coded-language-thug-bossy.

O'Dell, S. (1960). *Island of the blue dolphins*. New York, NY: Houghton Mifflin.

StopBullying.Gov, U.S. Department of Health and Human Services. (2017, September 24). *Diversity, Race and Religion*. Retrieved from www.stopbullying.gov/at-risk/groups/index.html.

Chapter 9

Utilizing Data for Systemic Change

In my first year as a school counselor, I attended a training led by my district. Each counselor received a CD of data. The CD had reports from many different sources and a massive spreadsheet for all 875 students in my school. I quickly became overwhelmed and never looked at the CD again. Fast forward to present day—massive spreadsheets still exist, but school counselors and their schools are getting more adept at using data as a tool for decision making that supports learning for all students.

It's important to consider good practices of systemic change so that your equity work can be the most effective possible. Utilizing data without planning for systemic change can be not only ineffective but dangerous. Attempts to intervene our way through equity gaps have historically failed, as seen by the persistent gap in achievement despite years of intervention in schools. Instead, we must think of the systems at work within our schools and create a plan that is feasible, effective, and sustainable. Often this will look and sound like conversations around instructional practices. In fact, excellent instruction **is** equity. When all students are learning in the way that they need and achieving their personal goals, we have equity in our system. In this chapter, we will look at the six principles of systemic change from *Systems Change: A Guide to What It Is and How to Do It* (Abercrombie, Harries, & Wharton, 2015) and the Positive Behavioral Interventions and Support (PBIS) Team-Initiated Problem Solving Model (TIPS) (Horner, et al., 2015) as tools for guiding your systemic change discussion.

Planning for Systems Change

Some quick tips to get you started:

- Identify the equity gap and determine which team or person has the power in that area.
- Find points of leverage to get on the agenda: think about the work of the team and speak to that purpose.
- Continue to guide the conversation about what you can control; for example, only complaining about state laws may not be the most effective use of your school's time.

Principle 1: Understand Needs and Assets

It may seem obvious that we want to work to understand the needs of students and the assets your school has to meet these needs. In fact, your school improvement team and administration spend a large amount of their time working on matching needs with assets. When we begin to look at this principle with an equity lens, we can see that students, families, and communities that are historically underserved may not have their needs or assets acknowledged in ways that the needs and assets of the majority are acknowledged.

We begin by looking at data to identify equity gaps but we can't assume that we, as a school, understand what the data means without asking our students and families. Imagine the power of asking, really asking, what is causing the greater number of absences, decreased achievement, or increased behavior concerns. At a school where I worked, we noticed that students who were recent immigrants to the country had a greater number of absences than students who were not. Our parent liaison and I took some time to chat with the parents of students who had recently immigrated and learned that school attendance was much more fluid in their countries of origin. This became even clearer when we had a big thunderstorm and our phone lines were flooded with calls from parents asking if we were having school that day. In countries where roads may not be paved and school houses may be open to the elements, a storm with hail and lightning might indeed cause school closure. A conversation with parents helped us to identify the assets that we possessed, buses and sturdy buildings, that allowed us to meet the needs of this group of students. We took the time to discuss the parents' concerns and explain that school buildings are often used as shelters for safety. The parents' concerns were resolved and attendance improved on stormy days.

When identifying assets, schools can also overlook the assets of populations that are judged to be less privileged. What assets do the communities of your students offer? At my school, the parents who had recently immigrated to the United States were also more likely to have one parent who stayed home with younger siblings. Many of these parents did not speak English but were available and willing to help around the school. The parent liaison and I worked together to personally invite parents to participate in a group of volunteers who could support the school in ways in which language did not factor. For instance, when a delivery of balloons for a balloon release arrived without bird-safe strings, we were able to call our group of volunteers who arrived en masse to help us at the last minute. This group also laminated posters, copied worksheets, and otherwise supported our teachers in their daily tasks. We were so thankful for their help, and an unintended positive consequence was that the parents felt much more incorporated in the community of the school.

When utilizing data for systemic change, it's important to not stop at the gaps you identify and jump right into interventions. Support is limited if you do not bring the voices of students alive so that you know what their needs really are. Meet these needs with a combination of assets from your school, the community at large, and, more importantly, the communities of your students.

Principle 2: Engage Multiple Actors

Identifying students' needs is the first step to systemic change in schools but the next step is equally crucial. We must engage all actors within our system, typically referred to as our "stakeholders." Who are the stakeholders in your building? Teachers, administration, non-certified staff, community organizations, and parents immediately come to mind. Who are the advocates, influencers, and resistors for equity within your stakeholders?

Our advocates for equity are typically fairly easy to identify. These adults work hard for all students. They speak up when they see inequity and support when they see equity. Depending on the climate of your building, these adults may or may not be influencers. Influencers are people that have power to affect other people and their thinking. Influencers are essential to systemic change because they spread the change throughout the system. Who does your principal listen to? Who elicits loyalty and trust from parents and community? Who holds the purse strings for the building and PTA budgets? These are your influencers.

Sometimes in systemic change overlooking resisters can be tempting. We assume they don't care about students needs. This is a mistake. In fact, we need to leverage our resisters as great sources of information about roadblocks for our work. Why do resisters behave the way that they do? Their answers will help us to be creative in our solutions. I once worked with a teacher who was completely against a schoolwide program that we were starting. This program was called Absolutely Incredible Kids® from Camp Fire USA (www.campfire.org) and involved parents writing a letter to their children. With 875 students we had many letters to collect and needed to make plans for students whose parents did not write a letter. It was, admittedly, a lot of work. She was very vocal about her opposition in meetings and in the break room. She and I had a positive working relationship, so I took the time to go and speak to her about her concerns. She shared that she was already overwhelmed with the amount of work that she had and didn't think she could take on any additional responsibilities. She was also worried that her students were below grade level and didn't need any instructional time taken away. Her gripes were loud and sometimes annoying but her concerns were valid.

I took this time in our conversation to ask clarifying questions and ensure that she felt heard and understood. I then asked if she was open to brainstorming some solutions to her concerns. We worked together to increase the support teachers were given in preparing the stationery to be sent home, following up with families who were missing letters, and ultimately writing letters for students who did not have a letter from their families. In the end, 100 percent of our students received a letter on Absolutely Incredible Kids® (AIK) Day. Over 90 percent of students received a letter from their families, including letters from other countries and even a few letters from incarcerated loved ones. It was a powerful day. Afterwards, the teacher made a point to come and thank me for not giving up on the idea. She said that the day helped her to see her students in the way that their parents saw them and that it brought her classroom community closer together.

Of course, I could have moved forward with the idea for AIK day without enrolling her support but I am glad that we had the conversation. In the end, her concerns made the experience better and naturally supported our future working relationship. You see, this teacher had taught at our school for a long time and had watched the school change from a more affluent, mostly white school to a high-poverty, "majority minority" school. She sometimes struggled with this change and her classroom environment (and student learning) suffered. I truly think that the combination of our conversation and the community building aspect of AIK day helped her to see her students not as "troublemakers" but as kids who want to learn and enjoy their learning. Berating teachers for their poor results without seeking to understand and engage won't get us better results. We have to take the time to engage all the stakeholders within our building in order to realize change at a systems level.

Principle 3: Map the System

The final principle for planning systems change is mapping the system. While this can sometimes mean creating a visual map of how stakeholders, processes, and institutions intertwine, that step is not typically necessary for a school. While looking at data, enrolling stakeholders, and listening to the needs of students and parents, you will likely find a pattern of concerns that need to be addressed in order to allow all students equity and access. In the mapping process of the system of the school, think about how stakeholders relate to each other, the beliefs and assumptions of stakeholders, and the different points of view that are commonly held. School climate surveys, teacher working conditions surveys, parent coffee chats, and professional learning community discussions are a great way to gain insight into describing the system of the school. In addition, it allows stakeholders to see the points of view of others within the building.

Once a description of the concerns and viewpoints of stakeholders are obtained, it is important to map the boundary of your system. Within every school, there are certain factors that cannot be eliminated: state and federal laws, district policies, personnel levels, budget, and mandatory testing are typically outside the purview of your school leadership. When faced with these boundaries, it is imperative that we do not stop, throw up our hands and cry unfair. Theodore Roosevelt stated in his autobiography: "There is a bit of a homely philosophy … which sums up one's duty in life: 'Do what you can, with what you've got, where you are'" (Roosevelt, 1913). The system can also change within these boundaries in order to eliminate inequities.

Doing the Work of Systems Change

Some quick tips to get you started:

- Don't do it alone—even if you are the only counselor.
- Be realistic about what you can change and start there.
- Clarify action steps, their purpose, and who is owning them.
- Keep learning from what works and doesn't work—if it doesn't work, stop and find a new focus.

Principle 4: Work with Others

Even when schools work hard to incorporate stakeholders in the planning for systems change, they can neglect to work with those within and outside the system in the actual work itself. Sometimes we fall into the trap of thinking that we can work more quickly and efficiently if we move forward independently. However, different stakeholders have access to different areas of power, different networks, and different assets. In one school where I worked, we wanted to support our Tier 2 behavior support students with stronger core behavior expectations and a better intervention process so that we could decrease the over-representation of African American males in our office referrals. The student services team had worked hard to create targeted "Closing the Gap" intervention plans that were successful for students who were targeted, but our overall gap did not decrease.

In looking at our data, the PBIS team had created an outstanding core framework for use school-wide but when we disaggregated the data, some teachers had not implemented with fidelity and were over-referring students for behavior difficulties that would have been mitigated with better core behavior instruction. Some teachers had a solid core but lacked a set of Tier 2 interventions that would support students in their behavior and avoid the need for an office discipline referral. If the student services team had worked alone, we would have received the same results we had always received—an improvement for targeted students but a continued widening of the gap in office discipline referrals for white students and students of color.

The counselors and the PBIS team worked together to create a Behavior Support Team (BST). The team would look at data for specific students, teachers, and grade levels. The BST could invite a teacher to come when the data indicated a need or the teacher could request a slot in the BST schedule. In the meeting, teachers, administrators, the counselor, and the psychologist helped teachers to create a plan to support their class. Each person on the team brought their own ideas, talents, and specialties to the conversation. It was also helpful for teachers to hear about behavior from someone other than the counselor and psychologist. Sometimes the buy-in was greater because teachers felt it was a peer brainstorming in collaboration rather than a specialist telling in isolation. Overall, our behavior office referrals decreased and the equity gap also decreased. We were able to keep more kids successfully in class learning.

Principle 5: Distribute Leadership

This principle may be more aptly described as "distribute ownership." In a school, the principal is the leader and the level of distributed leadership will vary based on their personal leadership style and philosophy. The school counselor might be able to advocate for change with the principal, but ultimately cannot change how the principal chooses to lead their building.

That said, the counselor has a leadership role within a school that they can use to distribute ownership over problems and solutions within the system. I worked in a school that had many children below grade level and that operated under the guise of intervention for everybody. The teachers were overwhelmed, students weren't improving and many were being retained. A group of teachers, student services, and interventionists on the intervention team decided that it would be helpful to put systems in place that allowed grade levels to support the intent of the work (helping more students to meet grade level expectations) while allowing them the autonomy to work as a team for improvement. Our school already implemented Professional Learning Communities (PLCs) but spent the PLC time discussing individuals rather than groups of students. This was not an effective use of time and there were invariably kids that fell off the agenda due to time constraints.

The intervention team worked together to create groups of students for each grade level at the beginning of the year. The criteria changed with age but might include a group of students who were below grade level in reading and had low fluency. Another group might be students who struggled with applying math concepts to word problems. The interventionists brought their in-depth knowledge of universal screeners and skills needed to master grade level work to create the lists. The grade levels enabled quick identification of groups of students to work with and choice of the best intervention for these students. The leadership was in the focus of the work but not in the details. As a result, our test scores improved immensely and we were able to achieve our goal of having more students meeting grade level expectations. How is this related to equity? We were no longer identifying and pinpointing "problem children" or students who seemed to need help, but were instead creating groups of students based on their actual skills and needs.

Principle 6: Foster a Learning Culture

Educators love to learn, so we must have a learning culture. Many schools have a culture of achievement and teachers or staff members who are not perceived to be achieving are blamed. When exciting new ideas come to your school through outside learning, how are these ideas received? Are staff members given the grace to try new things? The authors of *Systems Change* state: "A learning organisation is continually engaged in an iterative process of planning, doing, reviewing, and reflecting" (Abercrombie, Harries, and Wharton, 2015, p. 36). These are embedded in the ASCA National Model and, likely, in your school's professional growth plan or evaluation tool for staff. For systemic change, we must step outside of reflection and learning at an individual level and look to how we can reflect and adapt as a system.

To begin, encourage creativity and problem solving within your school teams. When you hear the phrase "But we've always done it this way," ask why. Avoid blame at all costs, even when discussing teachers or concerns during lunch or outside the building. Blame will eat away at the culture of your school and make staff members and students afraid. Once new ideas are shared and problem solving is occurring, create space for reflection as a regular practice. If you implement PLCs, leave time in the PLC for time to reflect and learn. If your school does not implement PLCs, consider ways that this time for reflection and learning can be embedded in your staff meetings, grade level/department planning, or leadership team. Often the counselor has the power to create agendas and set meeting items within their building. Think about your realm of influence and make these areas a place of learning culture.

I once worked in a building that was far from a learning culture. The staff was scared to make any decisions lest they be blamed for perceived mistakes by the principal. It was a hard place to work and students were negatively impacted. When I arrived, I quickly realized that a lot of work I was accustomed to doing would be widely resisted because of the culture of fear. Because of that, I worked to make the teams that I led places of support and learning. I created systems and procedures to make compliance concerns easy to understand. I allowed time for questions and comments. I asked my teams what they thought. I genuinely listened to their answers. I also allowed my teams to give feedback anonymously while they were building trust so that I could better understand what was needed. While I was not able to change the culture of the school overall, the teams that I led worked better and students benefited.

Utilizing Data

Now that you have thought conceptually about systemic change, it is time to utilize data to highlight where change needs to occur. When we look at a subgroup like race, we want to make sure that we are meeting students' needs rather than making an assumption about their needs based on their race. If your school has an achievement gap in achievement by race, what other layers of data can you use to ascertain what needs might be met? In the district where I work, a middle school noticed that the achievement gap on state mandated testing between white and nonwhite students was over 30 percentage points. Instead of identifying "at-risk" students based on undefined criteria or even race, they looked at first-quarter grades. All students who were failing a core class in the first quarter were nonwhite. They used a two layer strategy to determine which students, and even teachers, might need help or support in a way that would then narrow the achievement gap. Once they identified this group of students, they used the Team-Initiated Problem Solving (TIPS) Model to determine a root cause and create a plan for intervention that would support this targeted group of students. We will use this example as we walk through the TIPS model.

Team-Initiated Problem Solving

The pbis.org site has many TIPS materials that are free to download and instructional videos to support your team. This example is intended to support your equity work and is not a comprehensive explanation of the model.

Make Observations to Identify the Problem

The school counselors noticed a pattern in the students who were failing one or more courses in the first quarter, namely that they were more likely to be students of color. This aligned with the overall achievement gap that had been identified in their School Improvement Plan (SIP). The counselors were able to identify a target group that would support the SIP while only identifying students with an expressed area of need. In this part of the TIPS model, teams should stick only to the data and not try to hypothesize about what is contributing to the problem identified.

Write a Broad Problem Statement

Many teams skip over the step of writing a problem statement. They want to go directly to the SIP goal and start listing strategies. However, unless the broad problem statement is identified it is easy to get off course in the actual work that needs to happen. It's like the old saying "can't see the forest for the trees." For our example, the broad problem statement is that white students are more likely to pass state mandated testing than students of color and white students are more likely to pass all of their first-quarter classes than black students. While this broad statement hints at a possible causal relationship, we are not ready to make that assertion. There may be other factors at play.

Goal Alignment

The counselors aligned their program goal to the SIP so that all stakeholders would recognize the ways in which the counseling program supported the needs of the school. The SIP goal stated that test scores would rise for all students. The counselors' program goal was more focused:

By the end of the school year, 95 percent of sixth grade students who were failing one or more core class at first-quarter report cards will pass all core classes at final grades.

The program goal aligns with the SIP goal and allows the counselors to implement a variety of activities to support the goal. At this stage, the counselors have not determined which strategies will be the most helpful. They need to gather more data, or information, to be able to move forward.

Develop a Hypothesis

To create a hypothesis about what is causing students to fail core classes in the first quarter, the counselors attend the sixth grade PLC and lead a discussion about the specific students that have failed. The teachers respond that students lacked study skills and had never been taught how to study or to be an effective student. When the counselors look at feeder patterns for the school, the students failing were more likely to have come from high-poverty elementary schools where it is possible that they focused more on remediation than critical thinking skills.

When using data to create problem statements and hypotheses to discern root causes, it is important to look at instruction, curriculum, and environment before looking to the learner. What does this mean? Instruction is how the curriculum is taught. In this case, the students in sixth grade may not have been exposed to opportunities to be an effective student because their curriculum, what is taught, focused on remediation. Environment is where the instruction takes place. This includes structure, physical arrangement, distractions, peers, adults, and any other environmental factors that could affect learning. While exploring Instruction, Curriculum, Environment, and Learner (ICEL), it can be helpful to use the RIOT acronym: review, interview, observe, test. ICEL by RIOT matrices are widely available online through websites like interventioncentral.org and the Florida Problem Solving/Response to Intervention Project.

The counselors agree to move forward with the hypothesis that students are failing first-quarter classes because they have not yet been taught how to be active participants in school in ways that would improve their understanding of the content.

Write a Precise Problem Statement

The counselors added details to their broad problem statement to add clarity and understanding. The precise problem statement reads:

> While 60 percent of students are passing state mandated testing in reading, only 13 percent of black and 16 percent of hispanic students are passing. Of the students who are failing 1st quarter core classes, 100 percent are students of color. A discrepancy is evident in passing rates because students of color are more likely to come from a low performing elementary school where critical thinking skills may have been taught inadequately.

Discuss and Select Solutions

The counselors decided to implement a multi-pronged approach to supporting the students targeted in their program goal. The eighth grade counselor, who has worked in the district the longest and has formed a positive relationship with the elementary counselor from the Elementary School with students who are struggling in sixth grade, called the school to speak with the counselor and advocated for the increase in critical thinking study skills for rising sixth graders in the future.

The counseling team strategized that core lessons in critical thinking and study skills would support all students and may help to provide a baseline of knowledge for students who have not been exposed to the skills in a way that benefits them academically. In addition, they created a small group around academic achievement that supports students in setting learning goals, practicing study skills, and learning about how to self-select best practices in learning. Finally, the counseling team decided it might be helpful to split the list of students who failed first quarter and to check in on them weekly to create a strong relationship and help students to look at the scores on assignments and tests for reflection.

Develop and Implement an Action Plan

The ASCA National Model provides the "Closing the Gap" plan that can serve as the counselors' action plan for this work.

Evaluate and Revise Action Plan

In their weekly PLC meeting, the counselors pulled a failing list from the school database and checked in on students who were targeted by first-quarter grades. They discussed students who were successful and unsuccessful. When they looked at students who were not able to increase their grades, they also looked for patterns in teachers, teams, and subjects to determine if bias might play a part in the continued need of the student or students.

The counselors noticed that many of the students of color who continued to fail a core class despite the interventions in place were failing English/Language Arts (ELA). The counselors spoke with the ELA teachers, who shared that the school required teachers to teach from the same curriculum that had been used for years. The teachers were frustrated because the books were outdated and did not reflect the diverse population of students that attended the school. The counselors met with administration, who had previously dismissed the teachers' concerns as complaining, and showed them the data that showed that students were more likely to be failing ELA despite the interventions that had been put in place even when the same interventions were helping students in other courses. The counselors used data to advocate along with the ELA teachers for a more robust ELA curriculum that was engaging for all students.

In the following agenda we have included talking points and reflection questions to guide your system change discussion using data. We encourage you to set aside time to allow reflection and discussion as a team, whether that be your counseling PLC, advisory council, SIP team, or other team of problem solvers who are ready to interrupt racism in your school.

Agenda: Problem Solving for Equity

Purpose of the Meeting
Team will identify outcome data (achievement, attendance, or behavior) that show a significant gap between subgroups by race.

School Improvement Plan Review
- Are there SIP goals that reflect a gap in data by race?
- Has the SIP plan identified strategies that will be implemented?
- What part can school counselors play in the identified strategies?

Data Review
- Compare other data points that may reflect a gap not identified in your school improvement plan. For example: ACT scores.
- Identify additional layers of data that may inform the SIP goals. For example: first-quarter grades.

Discuss Importance and/or Feasibility of Addressing each Data Point
- Are there areas of extreme need that should be addressed first?
- What are your observations about what needs are the most concerning to stakeholders?
- What steps have you taken to gather input from stakeholders? If none, consider pausing the work until input is gathered.
- Are there areas of need that cannot be feasibly addressed? Why? Are you sure?

Select Data for a Problem Statement
- Choose two–four areas that show a significant equity gap and develop problem statements that reflect the gap for each.

Create a Hypothesis
- Addressing one area of need at a time, consider the reasons behind the gap that may be present.
- Are there instruction, curriculum, and environmental practices that might be contributing to the area of need?
- Are there systemic features that cause the identified gap?

Create a Plan
- Addressing one area of need at a time, develop a plan for action. Be specific with whom, what, when, and where each of the action steps will take place.
- Identify appropriate fidelity checks for each action step.
- Identify progress monitoring points for each area of data and a plan for ensuring that follow through occurs.

Pitfalls to Avoid

There are times when data is used to perpetuate inequity rather than to break it down. Chris Emdin reflects on the false narrative in working with students: "Our understandings of who was and wasn't a good student were rooted less in our experiences with urban students and more on our perceptions of them, which were largely based on a flawed narrative" (Emdin, 2016, p. 42). It is for this reason that we must avoid two pitfalls: the myth that working for all students helps all students and that data is infallible.

Working for All Does Not Help All

If we continue to look only at schoolwide data without disaggregating for race, the glaring inequities of our system will continue to stay hidden. In one large suburban high school I worked with, 16 percent of all students failed one or more courses in ninth grade. When looking at this overall number, it looks like over 80 percent of students are meeting core expectations so only Tier 2 and Tier 3 interventions are necessary. However, when data is disaggregated by race, 33 percent of black students, 29 percent of hispanic students, and 29 percent of multi-racial students failed a course in ninth grade. Clearly, the core instruction was effective for white students but not for students of color. Working for all did not support all students.

In another high school, 80 percent of white students scored a 22 or higher on the ACT while only 30 percent of black students did. When looking at the test scores for the same school 87 percent of students met grade level standards on state mandated testing with a small fluctuation in achievement when disaggregated by race. ACT scores are vital to being accepted into college. What was happening so that black students were performing similarly to white peers on the state mandated test and not on the ACT?

The failure to disaggregate by race leads to student needs being misidentified or missed so that students are not being supported in the way that they need. Ultimately, systems perpetuate the racial inequalities that have historically taken place.

Data is Not Infallible

When we rely on data as foolproof justification for policies and procedures, we can miss ways that data may fail to capture what is intended. In one elementary school, more than 80 percent of students were non-white but the vast majority of Academically and Intellectually Gifted students were white. The school system had a policy of testing all third graders using a standardized test so that teacher bias in referral for AIG testing was minimized. So why the discrepancy? I heard many people arguing poverty, lack of parent support, and other biased assumptions for the disparity.

When a new AIG teacher came to the school, they were alarmed at the gap in AIG identification and began to work with second graders to teach critical thinking and problem solving skills so that students would better understand what the standardized test for AIG identification was asking and how to go about solving the problems on the test. The number of students who were eligible for AIG following this Tier I strategy increased greatly. The gap between identification of white students and non-white students became much smaller. Rather than assuming that the test highlighted a racial difference in ability based either on racism or the assumption of systemic inequalities, the AIG teacher supported students in being exposed to the skills necessary to do well in the placement test. The students still had to be able to complete the tasks and show that they had the unique ability to think creatively to solve problems that exemplifies AIG students, but now all students were able to access this skill rather than only some students. The data for AIG identification in this case was not exposing a vast ability difference but simply an opportunity gap between students.

Points to Consider

- Ask, really ask, historically marginalized groups about equity gaps in data.
- Identify assets from all communities that can contribute to school success.
- Take the time to engage all stakeholders to realize change at a systems level, both in planning and in action steps.
- Distribute ownership over problems and solutions within the system.
- Honor the cycle of improvement, learning, and growing—including failure.
- Use layers of data and a problem solving process, like TIPS, to implement effective strategies and interventions.
- Working for all does not support all and data is fallible.

References

Abercrombie, R., Harries, E., & Wharton, R. (2015). *Systems change: A guide to what it is and how to do it.* London: New Philanthropy Capital.

Emdin, C. (2016). *For White folks who teach in the Hood … and the rest of y'all too: Reality pedagogy and urban education.* Boston, MA: Beacon Press.

Horner, R. H., Newton, J. S., Todd, A. W., Algozzine, B., Algozzine, K., Cusumano, D. L., & Preston, A. I. (2015). The Team-Initiated Problem Solving (TIPS II) training materials. Retrieved from www.TIPS2info.blogspot.com.

Roosevelt, Theodore. (1913). *An Autobiography.* New York: Macmillan; Bartleby.com, 1998.

Chapter 10

Change is Hard

Responding to Criticism and Pushback

Working for systemic change will likely result in criticism and pushback. As counselors, we often highly value consensus and collaboration but conflict is a necessary part of change. Being prepared for conflict can reduce feelings of anxiety. If you are a professional school counselor of color, you may also have feelings of tension, fear, and resentment. These feelings are normal and expected. Common coinciding feelings of hopefulness and anticipation may also surface. Professional school counselors of color, depending on the support of your school administrations and district, may even have justifiable concerns about job security should they take action to eradicate racism in their school. Counselors can take care to evaluate their school environment to balance their needs (for example, to remain employed) with the needs of the school community. Support systems can prove beneficial for professional school counselors of color particularly because of these vulnerabilities. Counselors may need increased diligence when recording and reporting any instances of retaliation, microaggressions, and/or overt racism. Self-care is especially crucial for communities that are particularly at risk of criticism and pushback.

If you are a white professional school counselor, it's important to reflect on your role as an ally. Allyship is not an identity. Rather, it's the process and the actions of working in solidarity with a marginalized group. That means the work of allyship is mostly about "unmarginalizing" those groups and reducing harm: learning to listen to students, staff, and parents of color and amplifying their voices by inviting them into power. Finally, it means educating yourself and other privileged people about the power and privilege that you get by not being marginalized in the same way. Consider this role of ally when you are planning to respond to criticism and pushback. Instead of getting into an argument with those who criticize you, continually come back to the purpose of your role as an ally and use this as your marker for action.

In the book *Crucial Conversations* (Patterson, 2012), the authors share their belief that two people, or a group of people, can talk about anything if all participants feel safe. As part of the ASCA Ethical Standards (ASCA, 2016), counselors are charged with developing and maintaining professional relationships and systems of communication with stakeholders to support students. While school counselors can and should be social activists for change within their building, they must do so in a way that does not damage relationships. This may differ than the way you handle interactions about race or equity outside the workplace. In personal spaces, you may be more inclined to unfollow, block, or end communication with acquaintances. Some people may even feel the need to end friendships altogether. While planning a school switch, Alicia chose to block access to her twitter feed. She felt it best to protect her tweets from potential employers who might judge her professionalism based on her activism before getting to know her as a counselor. We are not suggesting staying silent or not responding to racism or inequity when you see it because you don't want to rock the boat or because you don't want others to be uncomfortable. Carefully choose to embrace discomfort as necessary while also purposefully maintaining relationships with colleagues, students, parents, and community members.

Courageous Conversation Compass Protocol

To guide conversations about race and equity, we recommend the Courageous Conversations about Race Protocol (Singleton & Linton, 2006, pp. 58–65). The protocol starts with Four Agreements or norms:

- Stay engaged: remain in the conversation at all levels, be invested.
- Experience discomfort: stick with it—discomfort creates change.
- Speak your truth: be honest, don't say what you think others want to hear.
- Expect and accept non-closure: live in the uncertainty, don't rush to solutions.

In larger group conversations, these norms would be discussed and agreed upon before the conversation begins. Obviously, this will not happen in ad hoc, passing in the hallways, conversations, but school counselors have training in guiding group and individual conversations into purposeful, supportive dialogues. Use these skills to support the Four Agreements when possible. This can be hard to do in the middle of a challenging conversation. Be observant and prepare yourself by practicing your skills outside of the counseling office.

Courageous conversations are monitored and work to actively uphold the six conditions:

1. Focus on personal, local, and immediate.
2. Isolate race.
3. Normalize social construction and multiple perspectives.
4. Monitor agreements and establish parameter.
5. Use a working definition for race.
6. Examine the presence and role of whiteness.

These conditions could be a part of any staff meetings or professional learning opportunity within your building. However, the conditions will not be possible in every conversation with staff, parents, administrators, and students. In isolated conversations without established norms, concentrate your efforts on the first two conditions. Focus on the here and now and avoid broad, global generalizations by always speaking from a "place of I," beginning sentences with "I feel" or "I believe." Isolate race by talking about race explicitly and acknowledging that race influences the world and we cannot minimize its effect.

The courageous conversation about race protocol also includes a compass describing four ways that people deal with race: emotional, intellectual, moral, and social. The compass creates a framework for conversations and highlights the differences in the way that people converse, debate, or argue so that we can see others' perspectives as valuable.

Cultural Proficiency

When working with students, parents, and staff who have criticism of your work interrupting racism, it is helpful to reflect on their stage of cultural proficiency so that you can respond in the most appropriate way (Terrell & Lindsey, 2008).

- Cultural Destructiveness—seeking to assimilate or eliminate non-dominant cultures in schools.
- Cultural Incapacity—trivializing other cultures and making them seem inferior or wrong.
- Cultural Blindness—ignoring other cultures and their discrepant experiences in schools (e.g. as in the commonly offered statement, "I don't see color, I just see kids").
- Cultural Precompetence—beginning to realize your own ignorance and blindness and starting the journey towards learning with and about others.
- Cultural Competence—identifying the value of diversity and trying to align your educational practices with this value.
- Cultural Proficiency—engaging in ongoing learning about diversity issues in order to best serve the educational needs of all cultural groups.

In the cultural destructiveness stage, people are focused on assimilation. They do not view other cultures as equal to the dominant, white culture. They would prefer that others who are different align their identities with the mainstream. I have an acquaintance who laments that her black son refuses to associate with anything that he sees as "too black." His focus is on completely assimilating into white culture and to disown black culture altogether. In cultural incapacity, people trivialize other cultures and might see them as inferior or wrong. At a school that I work with, a teacher stated that black students should not be corrected for solving conflict through fighting because "that's how they resolve conflict in their culture." Broad assumptions and judgement are characteristics of these stages.

In the cultural blindness stage, people attempt to move beyond trivializing and demeaning other cultures by ignoring differences. This stage prevents the lived experiences of students from being recognized and can leave some students feeling unseen. In the cultural precompetence stage, people are beginning to realize that they have been ignorant and start the journey towards learning about others. One school counselor of color that I know shared that she remembers the first time that she experienced overt racism in the workplace. She stated that she knew that racism existed but had never really thought about how it impacted her. She now realized she had been impacted without even realizing it.

In the cultural competence stage, people value diversity and are working to align their practices with this value. Many teachers begin this work by creating diverse classroom libraries, reaching out to communities of color within their school communities, and checking lesson plans for cultural competencies. When people are culturally proficient, they know that they have just begun their work. They continually seek learning and understanding of people and cultures different than their own. They come to the work with a sense of questioning. When writing this book, the authors have been able to speak about and discuss our own understanding of cultural proficiency and have been constantly engaged in continual learning. At this level, culturally proficient educators are most comfortable with honest conversations without clear answers.

Alicia attended a professional development seminar at work at the beginning of the school year. Many new teachers had been hired to meet the increasing enrollment numbers at this predominantly black charter school. During the seminar about trauma-informed education in general, a new teacher inquired about overlooked resiliency in black traumatized children. His concern was that the trauma-informed model lacked a focus on student assets. He invited staff to consider the ways in which black students show support of each other despite hardship and are inclusive across difference. He is an example of a culturally proficient educator who was able to use presented information while offering deeper feedback related to race and culture.

Once you have begun to view the world with a culturally proficient lens, you can use your knowledge to respond to criticism and pushback in the most effective way.

Some Examples of Responses to Criticism

Example One

> You are a new school counselor at a large high school. You have been meeting with ninth grade teachers to discuss students who have a failing grade in first quarter. One of the teachers says in frustration: "Maybe these students would be doing better in school if they weren't so concerned about listening to their music loud in the parking lot and shouting at each other."

As culturally proficient counselors, you can see that this teacher is likely in the cultural destructiveness or incapacity stage, at least in this situation. You calmly ask her how she thinks that hanging out with friends and having fun is preventing students from doing well in school. She answers with more of the same. What would you do?

IDEAS TO CONSIDER

- Compassionate education is the answer here. This is a teachable moment where you can calmly discuss the holes in the assumptions that the teacher is making and create a new "story" for why some students are failing.
- Share the ways that having a positive peer group can help students to succeed in school.
- Take the time to determine actual causal factors, like poor study habits, that the school can mitigate in order to increase achievement.

Example Two

You are the MTSS liaison for the seventh grade. In your meetings, you discuss student data and look for patterns of success and areas of change. Your principal has asked you to disaggregate achievement data by racial subgroup and discuss with teachers the trends that you see in the grade level. When you present the information to the group, one teacher says to you: "I'm not sure why we need to talk about racial subgroups, if we are doing well by all students then every kid will learn."

You can see that this teacher is likely in the cultural blindness or precompetence stage. They are likely feeling uncomfortable talking about race because they realize that racial disparities exist within your school but aren't yet ready to explore the part that they play in it. What would you do?

IDEAS TO CONSIDER

- Curiosity is best in this conversation. Talk about the data that you are exploring and be curious about the trends that you see.
- Show compassion for the uncomfortableness of the conversation but persevere with the purpose of your work.
- Keep asking questions to unravel the misconceptions. Don't tell but lead to the truth.

Example Three

Your school improvement team is meeting to discuss your biannual school improvement goals. The gap in achievement between racial subgroups has been a topic of discussion and the team decides to focus their goals around the achievement gap. Your administrator is concerned because staff have had very little professional development on equity. She wants you to wait to implement strategies until all staff have had more training. You are concerned that this will delay the important work toward all students achieving equitably.

You identify your administrator as in the cultural proficiency stage. She knows that the work is just beginning. However, you also know that most of your staff are not there. You would prefer that the school work on cultural competence first. What would you do?

IDEAS TO CONSIDER

- Even talking about cultural proficiency and equitable practices is more than many are doing. Honor the work that has begun.
- When working with a group of people whose cultural competency levels differ widely, it's helpful to create concrete action items that are visible and measurable.

- Encourage your administrator to begin the work without waiting but to continue professional development at the same time. Cultural proficiency means that you know that your learning has just begun and will never end.
- Start somewhere and keep learning.

Barriers to Change

Social justice advocates will find common barriers to change: resistance, systems of oppression, sense of privilege and entitlement, and lack of understanding.

Resistance to change is a familiar barrier to school counselors. Change is hard and any change put in place will see pushback. This resistance is not a reflection of the purpose of the work for equity. Many people who resist change might fully support increased equity for students but struggle with making the changes necessary. When facing this type of resistance, it's usually best to respectfully listen and keep moving forward with the change. Think about the last time your school changed a type of technology that your staff was accustomed to. In my district, we recently changed email platforms and the level of complaining went through the roof. Before long, the way we used to do it will change into the way we do it now.

Example One

The counseling staff has decided to change the way that students elect to take AP courses. In the past, AP courses were listed within the registration system and students could choose a course with a sign off from the previous year's teacher. The counselors have decided that, in order to increase minority enrollment in AP courses, they will look at data to determine minority students who would be likely to succeed in AP courses. Within this targeted group of students, the counselors will conduct individual conferences and parent phone calls to encourage enrollment in AP courses. If minority students enroll in AP courses, the counselors will check in monthly to ensure students are doing well and to provide any support that they need to be successful. The science department has expressed concern about this change because it differs from the way that things "have always been done."

IDEAS TO CONSIDER

- Listen, listen, listen to the concerns of the Science department. They may have concerns that your department has not yet considered.
- Collect data and share it. With the support of your administrator, you can move forward even if you don't have full support from all teachers. Sometimes this is necessary, be prepared to share the results (positive and negative) so that stakeholders know that you are focused on improving student outcomes.
- Be transparent. Share the process with teachers. For example, in the weekly check-ins, counselors could follow up with AP teachers, within limits of confidentiality, about the goals of the students and areas where they are seeking additional support.

Systems of oppression can be nuanced and difficult to identify. Key indicators of systems of oppression include opportunity hoarding, where only those with knowledge and self-advocacy skills can access, and standardized requirements that leave no room for modifications based on need.

Example Two

You work at a magnet middle school that offers a wide variety of elective options, some of which require auditions. Students at your feeder elementary schools can sign up for any elective they choose but if they do not audition, they will not be placed in the class. You want to discontinue auditions but were told by the administration that is not possible.

IDEAS TO CONSIDER

- Review the standards: Are the required auditions necessary for success in the elective? For instance, advanced orchestra would require a level of skill to participate with other advanced musicians. However, yearbook team could be modified to fit the skills and learning needs of many students.
- Investigate: Go to the elementary schools and determine interest levels in the electives that require auditions. Are there students that have interest but choose not to register because they cannot audition? How many students register but never make it to an audition? Are certain communities disproportionately affected by the audition rule because they are further away from the middle school or lack public transportation?
- Advocate: Meet with electives instructors and administration to advocate for the removal of the audition requirement for all but the most necessary courses. Be prepared to respond to pushback with information collected during your review of standards and investigations.
- Remove Barriers: Determine ways to allow all students with an interest to audition. Can auditions take place at the elementary schools? By video? In community centers for communities further away from the school? Removing barriers can be inconvenient, be ready to enlist allies to support these efforts.

A sense of privilege and entitlement may be a barrier to change because communities may not want to relinquish the privilege that they have held. "When you are accustomed to privilege, equality feels like oppression" (Unknown). Privilege also means not having to think about others' problems.

Example Three

In a PTA meeting, the school is discussing how to use funds that were raised in excess of the adopted PTA budget. One group has asked the PTA to honor the diversity of the school by hosting speakers from cultures represented in the student body. A member of the PTA board has asked why white culture wasn't represented in the proposal.

IDEAS TO CONSIDER

- Listen: Ask the PTA member what that speaker would speak about. They may have a valuable idea that wasn't presented in the best way. For example, a white speaker who talks about a community interest like rain in a farming town or ships in a naval community.
- Ask Questions: If the PTA member continues to insist that they would like a speaker to talk about white culture, ask questions. Focus on what students would learn from the speaker.
- Share your concerns: This is where you can share your knowledge of students as a school counselor. Share your concerns about how groups of students will feel when the dominant culture is highlighted in an event that was intended to bring out the diversity of the student body.
- Find a solution: It may not be wise to simply put your foot down and refuse to acknowledge the PTA board member's request. Think about some solutions that will incorporate some of their ideas without causing your students of color to feel alienated or patronized.

Lack of understanding may seem like a blameless barrier to change but it is still an important barrier to address. Different adults and students may not have explored racial inequities and institutional racism at the same level. Because of this, there may be a barrier to change because your stakeholders do not understand the importance of the change.

In your School Improvement Team meeting, your team is looking at the disproportionality of out-of-school suspensions and office discipline referrals for black students. The team sees that black students are much more likely to be referred to the office and then to be suspended. One team member suggests looking more deeply at the incidents to determine if they were justified referrals and suspensions. When your team does this, you see that the referrals are truly based on major infractions of school policy. The team wants to end the discussion there with the idea that the disproportionality is inevitable because of student differences in conduct.

IDEAS TO CONSIDER

- More data is needed to respond to this decision. Ask the team if they are open to tabling the discussion so that more data can be collected.
- There are likely two causes for this disproportionality. One is that black students are more likely to be referred to the office and white students are more likely to remain in class without a referral. The other cause could be that the level of student engagement and mutual respect between students and teachers is not present to the extent needed for success.
- Talk with staff members, parents, students, and teachers to determine if there is a consensus on where the breakdown is.
- Refuse to agree that disproportionality is inevitable. Absolving the responsibility to close gaps is a fixed mindset and reflective of biased thinking. If the SIP team chooses to move on from the discussion in spite of your advocacy,

create an ASCA National Model "Closing the Gap" plan to address dispro-portionality in major office referrals and address the need as a school coun-selor or counseling department.

In your advisory council, you share your "Closing the Gap" plan to work with students of color to enroll in AP courses and to support their academic success while enrolled. A member of your advisory council asks: "Why are we looking at only minority students? I don't see color and I am uncomfort-able with you calling out minority students. Shouldn't we be helping all children?"

IDEAS TO CONSIDER

- This is an opportunity for education and compassionate conversation. Affirm the member's desire to help all students and show her the data that shows that students of color are less likely to enroll in AP courses.
- Ask how the member would suggest that white students could benefit from a similar program. It is true that school counselors work with all students and if there is a demonstrated need for certain subgroups of white students to be supported in a similar fashion, then perhaps the plan can be expanded.
- Continue with your good work and be ready to share your successes at the end of the year. This type of pushback doesn't need to derail your plan.

Justice Fatigue

Actively working for change can be exhausting. Once we see the injustices inherit in our systems, it can't be unseen. Constantly being exposed to injustice can cause fatigue in social activists, particularly for those of color. Add to that, school counselors often battle compassion fatigue, or secondary stress reaction, from supporting students and families that have been traumatized or are under significant emotional distress. The combination of justice fatigue (working for systemic change in the structures of the school) and compassion fatigue (indi-vidual and family work around trauma and highly emotional life events) can lead to burnout.

The symptoms of professional fatigue might include:

- Feeling overwhelmed by the enormity of the issues being faced.
- Chronic emotional or physical exhaustion.
- Feelings of self-contempt (why can't I do more?).
- Irritability.
- Depersonalization of students, families, and teachers.

When you see these symptoms in yourself or your colleagues, it is time to act. You can't be an agent of change when you are on the fast track to burnout. Self care isn't just bubble baths and long massages. Taking care of your physical and emotional health are crucial to being an effective school counselor.

Make Things Easier

Prepare, prepare, prepare. Reduce the cognitive load of your work any way that you can. This might include letting go of activities or responsibilities that don't add value to your big areas of work. If your big goals are equity and social justice, the monthly bulletin boards that you usually do can probably go if they don't add value to your work. If your big goals are students' social emotional learning, do you really need to do quarterly attendance awards? Bus duty is probably still on your list, but cut what you can.

Take Care of Your Physical Needs

Create a goal for your physical needs every month, semester, or school year. These are not goals related to body image or even health but are really about your physical needs at work and at home. One year my goal was to eat lunch before dismissal, another year my goal was to work no more than nine-hour days. These goals weren't going to set records for changing my overall health but they helped me to take care of my physical needs to prevent burnout.

Have Fun

Choose fun activities with your students and colleagues. Having fun together keeps work satisfaction high and releases those good endorphins. If you and a colleague are having a disagreement over an injustice that you are working to change, it's easier to do that respectfully when you played ultimate frisbee last week.

Find Your Tribe

There are other people in your building who are social justice warriors too. If there aren't, spread your reach to other school counselors in your district or through social media channels such as Facebook, Twitter, and Instagram. Spend enough time with them so that every conversation isn't about teaching and understanding equity. You understand each other, and that makes a big difference.

When You Feel Stuck

I once worked in a school where I was constantly exposed to systemic injustices that seemed around every corner. I began my time there sure that I would be an agent of change. However, due to the community, district systems, and a lack of distributed leadership, I soon began to feel like I was part of the problem. I had to decide: Do I stay or do I go?

This is a personal decision and no-one but you can decide what's best for you. For me, I tried to get "unstuck" in a variety of ways: self-care, advocacy, finding like-minded colleagues. However, in the end, I couldn't stay. I sometimes feel guilt that I left. However, I also know that I am only effective when I am at my best and the job was not a healthy place for me to be. I truly believe that if I had stayed, I would have left the profession broken and cynical. Once I left, I was able to spread my interests and take on new challenges, ultimately, I believe, creating a bigger ripple of change for good. When I am in my most self-compassionate state, I can acknowledge that I left changes behind that continue to support kids.

There are times when equity work for systemic change will feel like three steps forward and two steps back. Take the time to make your response to criticism and pushback about continuing both the work and your own wellbeing. You are best at helping others when you feel supported, impactful, and healthy.

Points to Consider

- Conflict is a necessary part of change, be prepared and consider your needs as a school counselor of color or a white ally.
- Place high value on participant's feeling of safety in order to maintain professional relationships and systems of communication to support students.
- Use the courageous conversation protocol to create conditions for open dialogue.
- Consider the cultural proficiency level of those involved to inform your response.
- Common barriers to change are: resistance to change, systems of oppression, sense of privilege and entitlement, and lack of understanding.
- Practice self-care in the face of struggle.

References

American School Counselor Association. (2016). *ASCA ethical standards for school counselors*. Alexandria, VA: Author.

Patterson, Kerry. (Eds.) (2012). *Crucial conversations: Tools for talking when stakes are high*. New York: McGraw-Hill.

Singleton, Glenn E., & Linton, Curtis. (2006). *Courageous Conversations about Race: A Field Guide for Achieving Equity in Schools*. Thousand Oaks, CA: Corwin.

Terrell, Raymond D., & Lindsey, Randall B. (2008). *Culturally Proficient Leadership*. Thousand Oaks, CA: Corwin.

Celebrating Diversity Book List

Picture Books

Same, Same but Different by Jenny Sue Kostecki-Shaw
> The book is a comparison of the cultures of two children who are penpals from America and India. They do the same things (like ride the bus, be outside, have families), but they do them in different ways.

It's OK to be Different by Todd Parr
> A book about feeling in good spirits no matter who you are!

Sneetches by Dr. Seuss
> This is not only a book about diversity, but also about changing oneself to fit in. Some Sneetches believe that they are the superior Sneetch because of their stars, but after spending all of their money to remain different, all the Sneetches realize the stars do not really matter.

Giraffes Can't Dance by Giles Andreae
> Other jungle animals convince Giraffe that he cannot dance and his feelings are hurt. But a few empathetic friends show Giraffe that he/she can dance to their own music.

Chocolate Milk, Por Favor by Maria Dismondy
> A story of a Spanish-speaking boy who comes to an American school where only English is spoken. At first, one white boy will not accept him, but eventually the two boys bond over a love of chocolate milk and soccer. It is a story directly about empathy and diversity.

The Name Jar by Yangsook Choi
> A little girl just moved from Korea to America and is afraid that no one will be able to pronounce her name, so she decides to let the kids give her name suggestions. One of her classmates finds out her actual name and its meaning and decides to hide the name jar, so Unhei will tell everyone her real name.

Malala's Magic Pencil by Malala Yousafzai
> The true story of Malala, a schoolgirl who was shot by the Taliban and survived. This is her story in kid-friendly language sharing all the power of writing and standing up for something.

Jabari Jumps by Gaia Cornwall
> About having the courage to do something new (in this case, jumping off the diving board). The main character, Jabari, is an African American boy.

Charlotte and the Quiet Place by Deborah Sosin
> Charlotte, an African American girl, takes a moment in a noisy city to find a calming place

Hidden Figures: The True Story of Four Black Women and the Space Race by Margot Lee Shetterly
> The story of four black women who played a vital role in the United States' success in the space race. Picture-book version of the biography and movie.

Ada Twist, Scientist by Andrea Beaty
> Shatters the stereotypes that girls, and black girls in particular, are not interested in science!

I am Harriet Tubman by Brad Meltzer
> Tells the story of Harriet Tubman and her pivotal role in the fight against slavery through the Underground Railroad.

Let's Talk about Race by Julius Lester
> Explores what makes each of us special and introduces race as one of many parts of a person's identity.

Strictly No Elephants by Lisa Mantchev
> A boy and his pet elephant want to be a part of a pet club—but the problem is the pet club does not allow elephants. The boy starts his own club that is inclusive to everyone.

The Barefoot Book of Earth Tales by Dawn Casey and Anne Wilson
> Based on a true story of the Bishnoi tribes in India, the book takes you on the journey of social justice as a tribe stands up against people cutting down their trees in order to protect their village.

Separate is Never Equal by Duncan Tonatiuh
> The story of a lawsuit brought by Sylvia Mendez's family a decade before Brown v. Board of Education when Sylvia and her brothers were forced to attend the "Mexican school" instead of the school closest to her house. Her father fights for her rights and she is able to go to her closest school.

Can I Play Too? by Mo Willems
> Piggie and Elephant learn that they have to adapt the game so their friend, Snake, can play too.

Three Best Friends and Me, Zulay by Cari Best
> Zulay is blind and does not like using her cane. But with the help of her friends, she embraces who she is and takes part in field day.

Just Because by Rebecca Elliot
> A brother narrates the things that his big sister likes to do. As the story unfolds, the reader realizes that his sister has special needs.

The Youngest Marcher by Cynthia Levinson
> Audrey Faye Hendricks was the youngest child ever to be arrested during the civil rights protests in Birmingham, AL in 1963.

My Brother Charlie by Holly Robinson Peete and Ryan Elizabeth Peete
> Callie talks about her brother, Charlie, who has autism, and the similarities and differences they have.

Thank You, Mr. Falker by Patricia Polacco
> A story about a little girl with dyslexia who struggles academically until a teacher helps her to bring out her strengths.

Four Feet, Two Sandals by Karen Lynn Williams and Khadra Mohammed
> This is a story about two girls in a Pakistan refugee camp and their experience.

The Colour of Home by Mary Hoffman and Karin Littlewood
> The story of a little boy, Hassan, who flees from Africa to America to escape war. He doesn't understand English and is homesick. He begins to tell his story through artwork.

Grace for President by Kelly DiPucchio
> A great book to explain elections. An African American girl named Grace is determined to become the first female president.

Last Stop on Market Street by Matt de la Peña
> A book to inspire empathy in children as a little boy gets on a bus with his grandma and wonders why he doesn't have certain luxuries in the world.

I am Enough by Grace Byers
> This book has a positive message about embracing and loving who you are. The book is not about race but includes an African American girl on the cover and diversity in the illustrations.

Brave Girl: Clara and the Shirtwaist Masters' Strike of 1909 by Michelle Markel
> Based on a true story, Clara, a Ukranian immigrant, perseveres against horrible working conditions in the garment industry to lead the largest strike of women workers.

This Little Trailblazer by Joan Holub
> Board book that introduces influential women who changed history and explores the idea that trailblazers cause "big great changes."

Chapter Books

Wonder by R. J. Palacio
>August, a child with a face deformity, navigates the world of middle school—bullies, friendships, and feelings. Released as a movie in 2017.

Blubber by Judy Blume
>A book about effects of bullying without a feel good ending, but a lesson in compassion and caring about people.

El Deafo by Cece Bell
>A graphic novel about the experiences of being deaf.

Freedom Over Me by Ashley Bryan
>Poems written by a contemporary author inspired by the will of a plantation owner that lists the worth of his slaves. Bryan imagines the lives of the people on the plantation, including their dreams and pride in knowing that they were worth more than their owner would ever guess.

West Meadows Detectives: The Case of the Snack Snatcher by Liam O'Donnell
>The school cafeteria keeps getting trashed and snacks are being stolen! Myron, who has autism, has a special power of being able to catch clues that others are missing because his world is black and white.

Jaden Toussaint, the Greatest. Episode 1: The Quest for Screen Time by Marti Dumas
>Jaden, an African American boy, plans to convince his parents that he should have more screen time using science. From an Amazon review: "As a black parent, it's refreshing to read a book that's NOT about stereotypically black interests, racism, or urban life."

Cilla Lee-Jenkins: Future Author Extraordinaire by Susan Tan
>Cilla writes about herself. Some stories are funny, like how she dealt with being bald until she was five. Others are more poignant, like how she overcame her struggles with reading and how family traditions with her Jenkins family and her Chinese family are so different. All of her stories are filled with love and humor.

Flying Lessons and Other Stories edited by Ellen Oh.
>A compilation of famous children's authors' short stories about the uniqueness and universality in all of us. The *Time* review says: "… will resonate with any kid who's ever felt different—which is to say, every kid."

Forget Me Not by Ellie Terry
>Calliope has Tourette syndrome. She's also an interesting person and a good friend. Her neighbor, a popular kid, has to decide if he is brave enough to take their friendship public. A book about being true to oneself.

Ghost by Jason Reynolds

Four kids are chosen by an elite middle-school track team. Ghost is running from his past, including an abusive father. Their coach is determined to keep the kids from blowing their shots at life like he did.

I Will Always Write Back by Caitlin Alifirenka, Martin Ganda, and Liz Welch

An American girl and a boy from Zimbabwe become unlikely best friends after an assignment brings them together as penpals. A dual memoir that inspires readers to wonder about the world at large.

The Red Pencil by Andrea Davis Pinkney

Amira's life in a peaceful Sudanese village is changed forever when the Janjaweed attack. She makes the long journey, on foot, to safety at a refugee camp, a tough place to be until the gift of a red pencil opens up all kinds of possibilities.

Save Me a Seat by Sarah Weeks and Gita Varadarajan

Two boys, one white and one Indian American, support each other as they navigate middle school, family, and friendship.

Books for Teachers

For White Folks Who Teach in the Hood … and the Rest of Y'all Too: Reality Pedagogy and Urban Education by Chris Emdin

Brings together real life stories and theory, research, and practice. A new approach to teaching and learning for urban education drawing from the author's experience of feeling undervalued and invisible in classrooms as a young man of color and then a science educator.

The Dreamkeepers: Successful Teachers of African American Children by Gloria Ladson-Billings

Now in its second edition, the author revisits eight teachers who were profiled in the first edition and introduces readers to new teachers as exemplars of good teaching. Ladson-Billings shows that what matters most is the teacher's efforts to work with the strengths each child brings to the classroom.

Culturally Responsive Teaching and the Brain: Promoting Authentic Engagement and Rigor Among Culturally and Linguistically Diverse Students by Zaretta Hammond

Combines neuroscience research and culturally responsive instruction to share ten "key moves" to build students' learner operating systems and prepare them to be independent learners.

I'm Still Here: Black Dignity in a World Made for Whiteness by Austin Channing Brown

A memoir written by a black female named Austin so that future employers would think she was a white male. Austin explores what it's like to be black in her predominantly white community growing up and how she learned what it means to "love blackness."

School Counseling to Close the Achievement Gap: A Social Justice Framework by Cheryl Holcomb-McCoy
> A practical guide for school counselors rooted in the principles of social justice. Learn about incorporating data and increasing advocacy to close the achievement gap.

Multiplication is for White People: Raising Expectations for Other People's Children by Lisa Delpit
> There is no achievement gap at birth; this book describes the striking elements of public education that work against poor children of color. Includes stories from the classroom and outlines a blueprint for raising expectations for other people's children.

Pushout: The Criminalization of Black Girls in School by Monique W. Morris
> Black girls make up 16 percent of the nation's student body but more than one-third of all girls with a school-related arrest. This book tells the story of black girls across the country that have been pushed out of school.

Why Are All the Black Kids Sitting Together in the Cafeteria? by Beverly Daniel Tatum
> Is racial self-segregation a problem to be addressed or a coping strategy? This book discusses how straight talk about race is the only way communication can happen across racial divides.

Films and Documentaries about Celebrating Diversity

"13th," a documentary by Ava Duvernay
> Experts discuss the criminal justice system and the effects of bias on law enforcement. A history of law enforcement and the civil rights movement is explored and scrutinized by historians, legal experts, and formerly incarcerated individuals.

"American Promise," a documentary by Joe Brewster and Michele Stephenson
> The story about two young black male students who enter a predominantly white private school in New York City. Both boys take different paths with different outcomes although their treatment in school is almost identical.

"Dear White People," a film and series by Justin Simien
> The original film is about a black male student arriving on campus. The predominantly white university is surface-level inclusive. Throughout the course of the semester the young journalist learns the deeper levels of tension amongst students and faculty alike.

"I Am Not Your Negro," a docufilm by Raoul Peck
> Author James Baldwin helps narrate the story of the assassinations of civil rights leaders. Famous interviews about race, politics, and nationalism are shown through the lens of the storyteller.

Appendix B

Teaching Tolerance
Social Justice Standards

Table AB.1 Anchor Standards and Domains

Identity	Diversity
1. Students will develop positive social identities based on their membership in multiple groups in society. 2. Students will develop language and historical and cultural knowledge that affirm and accurately describe their membership in multiple identity groups. 3. Students will recognize that people's multiple identities interact and create unique and complex individuals. 4. Students will express pride, confidence, and healthy self-esteem without denying the value and dignity of other people. 5. Students will recognize traits of the dominant culture, their home culture, and other cultures and understand how they negotiate their own identity in multiple spaces.	6. Students will express comfort with people who are both similar to and different from them and engage respectfully with all people. 7. Students will develop language and knowledge to accurately and respectfully describe how people (including themselves) are both similar to and different from each other and others in their identity groups. 8. Students will respectfully express curiosity about the history and lived experiences of others and will exchange ideas and beliefs in an open-minded way. 9. Students will respond to diversity by building empathy, respect, understanding, and connection. 10. Students will examine diversity in social, cultural, political, and historical contexts rather than in ways that are superficial or oversimplified.

Justice	Action
11. Students will recognize stereotypes and relate to people as individuals rather than representatives of groups.	16. Students will express empathy when people are excluded or mistreated because of their identities and concern when they themselves experience bias.
12. Students will recognize unfairness on the individual level (e.g. biased speech) and injustice at the institutional or systemic level (e.g. discrimination).	17. Students will recognize their own responsibility to stand up to exclusion, prejudice, and injustice.
13. Students will analyze the harmful impact of bias and injustice on the world, historically and today.	18. Students will speak up with courage and respect when they or someone else has been hurt or wronged by bias.
14. Students will recognize that power and privilege influence relationships on interpersonal, intergroup, and institutional levels and consider how they have been affected by those dynamics.	19. Students will make principled decisions about when and how to take a stand against bias and injustice in their everyday lives and will do so despite negative peer or group pressure.
15. Students will identify figures, groups, events, and a variety of strategies and philosophies relevant to the history of social justice around the world.	20. Students will plan and carry out collective action against bias and injustice in the world and will evaluate what strategies are most effective.

Table AB.2 K-2 Grade Level Outcomes

Anchor Standard	Code	Grade Level Outcome
Identity 1	ID.K-2.1	I know and like who I am and can talk about my family and myself and name some of my group identities.
Identity 2	ID.K-2.2	I can talk about interesting and healthy ways that some people who share my group identities live their lives.
Identity 3	ID.K-2.3	I know that all my group identities are part of me—but that I am always ALL me.
Identity 4	ID.K-2.4	I can feel good about myself without being mean or making other people feel bad.
Identity 5	ID.K-2.5	I see that the way my family and I do things is both the same as and different from how other people do things, and I am interested in both.
Diversity 6	DI.K-2.6	I like being around people who are like me and different from me, and I can be friendly to everyone.
Diversity 7	DI.K-2.7	I can describe some ways that I am similar to and different from people who share my identities and those who have other identities.
Diversity 8	DI.K-2.8	I want to know about other people and how our lives and experiences are the same and different.
Diversity 9	DI.K-2.9	I know everyone has feelings, and I want to get along with people who are similar to and different from me.

continued

Table AB.2 Continued

Anchor Standard	Code	Grade Level Outcome
Diversity 10	DI.K-2.10	I find it interesting that groups of people believe different things and live their daily lives in different ways.
Justice 11	JU.K-2.11	I know my friends have many identities, but they are always still just themselves.
Justice 12	JU.K-2.12	I know when people are treated unfairly.
Justice 13	JU.K-2.13	I know some true stories about how people have been treated badly because of their group identities, and I don't like it.
Justice 14	JU.K-2.14	I know that life is easier for some people and harder for others and the reasons for that are not always fair.
Justice 15	JU.K-2.15	I know about people who helped stop unfairness and worked to make life better for many people.
Action 16	AC.K-2.16	I care about those who are treated unfairly.
Action 17	AC.K-2.17	I can and will do something when I see unfairness—this includes telling an adult.
Action 18	AC.K-2.18	I will say something or tell an adult if someone is being hurtful, and will do my part to be kind even if I don't like something they say or do.
Action 19	AC.K-2.19	I will speak up or do something if people are being unfair, even if my friends do not.
Action 20	AC.K-2.20	I will join with classmates to make our classroom fair for everyone.

Table AB.3 3–5 Grade Level Outcomes

Anchor Standard	Code	Grade Level Outcome
Identity 1	ID.3–5.1	I know and like who I am and can talk about my family and myself and describe our various group identities.
Identity 2	ID.3–5.2	I know about my family history and culture and about current and past contributions of people in my main identity groups.
Identity 3	ID.3–5.3	I know that all my group identities are part of who I am, but none of them fully describes me and this is true for other people too.
Identity 4	ID.3–5.4	I can feel good about my identity without making someone else feel badly about who they are.
Identity 5	ID.3–5.5	I know my family and I do things the same as and different from other people and groups, and I know how to use what I learn from home, school, and other places that matter to me.

Anchor Standard	Code	Grade Level Outcome
Diversity 6	DI.3–5.6	I like knowing people who are like me and different from me, and I treat each person with respect.
Diversity 7	DI.3–5.7	I have accurate, respectful words to describe how I am similar to and different from people who share my identities and those who have other identities.
Diversity 8	DI.3–5.8	I want to know more about other people's lives and experiences, and I know how to ask questions respectfully and listen carefully and non-judgmentally.
Diversity 9	DI.3–5.9	I feel connected to other people and know how to talk, work, and play with others even when we are different or when we disagree.
Diversity 10	DI.3–5.10	I know that the way groups of people are treated today, and the way they have been treated in the past, is a part of what makes them who they are.
Justice 11	JU.3–5.11	I try and get to know people as individuals because I know it is unfair to think all people in a shared identity group are the same.
Justice 12	JU.3–5.12	I know when people are treated unfairly, and I can give examples of prejudice words, pictures, and rules.
Justice 13	JU.3–5.13	I know that words, behaviors, rules, and laws that treat people unfairly based on their group identities cause real harm.
Justice 14	JU.3–5.14	I know that life is easier for some people and harder for others based on who they are and where they were born.
Justice 15	JU.3–5.15	I know about the actions of people and groups who have worked throughout history to bring more justice and fairness to the world.
Action 16	AC.3–5.16	I pay attention to how people (including myself) are treated, and I try to treat others how I like to be treated.
Action 17	AC.3–5.17	I know it's important for me to stand up for myself and for others, and I know how to get help if I need ideas on how to do this.
Action 18	AC.3–5.18	I know some ways to interfere if someone is being hurtful or unfair, and will do my part to show respect even if I disagree with someone's words or behavior.
Action 19	AC.3–5.19	I will speak up or do something when I see unfairness, and I will not let others convince me to go along with injustice.
Action 20	AC.3–5.20	I will work with my friends and family to make our school and community fair for everyone, and we will work hard and cooperate in order to achieve our goals.

Table AB.4 6–8 Grade Level Outcomes

Anchor Standard	Code	Grade Level Outcome
Identity I	ID.6–8.1	I know and like who I am and can comfortably talk about my family and myself and describe our various group identities.
Identity 2	ID.6–8.2	I know about my family history and culture and how I am connected to the collective history and culture of other people in my identity groups.
Identity 3	ID.6–8.3	I know that overlapping identities combine to make me who I am and that none of my group identities on their own fully defines me or any other person.
Identity 4	ID.6–8.4	I feel good about my many identities and know they don't make me better than people with other identities.
Identity 5	ID.6–8.5	I know there are similarities and differences between my home culture and the other environments and cultures I encounter, and I can be myself in a diversity of settings.
Diversity 6	DI.6–8.6	I interact with people who are similar to and different from me, and I show respect to all people.
Diversity 7	DI.6–8.7	I can accurately and respectfully describe ways that people (including myself) are similar to and different from each other and others in their identity groups.
Diversity 8	DI.6–8.8	I am curious and want to know more about other people's histories and lived experiences, and I ask questions respectfully and listen carefully and non-judgmentally.
Diversity 9	DI.6–8.9	I know I am connected to other people and can relate to them even when we are different or when we disagree.
Diversity 10	DI.6–8.10	I can explain how the way groups of people are treated today, and the way they have been treated in the past, shapes their group identity and culture.
Justice 11	JU.6–8.11	I relate to people as individuals and not representatives of groups, and I can name some common stereotypes I observe people using.
Justice 12	JU.6–8.12	I can recognize and describe unfairness and injustice in many forms including attitudes, speech, behaviors, practices, and laws.
Justice 13	JU.6–8.13	I am aware that biased words and behaviors and unjust practices, laws, and institutions limit the rights and freedoms of people based on their identity groups.
Justice 14	JU.6–8.14	I know that all people (including myself) have certain advantages and disadvantages in society based on who they are and where they were born.
Justice 15	JU.6–8.15	I know about some of the people, groups, and events in social justice history and about the beliefs and ideas that influenced them.

Anchor Standard	Code	Grade Level Outcome
Action 16	AC.6–8.16	I am concerned about how people (including myself) are treated and feel for people when they are excluded or mistreated because of their identities.
Action 17	AC.6–8.17	I know how to stand up for myself and for others when faced with exclusion, prejudice, and injustice.
Action 18	AC.6–8.18	I can respectfully tell someone when his or her words or actions are biased or hurtful.
Action 19	AC.6–8.19	I will speak up or take action when I see unfairness, even if those around me do not, and I will not let others convince me to go along with injustice.
Action 20	AC.6–8.20	I will work with friends, family, and community members to make our world fairer for everyone, and we will plan and coordinate our actions in order to achieve our goals.

Table AB.5 9–12 Grade Level Outcomes

Anchor Standard	Code	Grade Level Outcome
Identity 1	ID.9–12.1	I have a positive view of myself, including an awareness of and comfort with my membership in multiple groups in society.
Identity 2	ID.9–12.2	I know my family history and cultural background and can describe how my own identity is informed and shaped by my membership in multiple identity groups.
Identity 3	ID.9–12.3	I know that all my group identities and the intersection of those identities create unique aspects of who I am and that this is true for other people too.
Identity 4	ID.9–12.4	I express pride and confidence in my identity without perceiving or treating anyone else as inferior.
Identity 5	ID.9–12.5	I recognize traits of the dominant culture, my home culture, and other cultures, and I am conscious of how I express my identity as I move between those spaces.
Diversity 6	DI.9–12.6	I interact comfortably and respectfully with all people, whether they are similar to or different from me.
Diversity 7	DI.9–12.7	I have the language and knowledge to accurately and respectfully describe how people (including myself) are both similar to and different from each other and others in their identity groups.
Diversity 8	DI.9–12.8	I respectfully express curiosity about the history and lived experiences of others and exchange ideas and beliefs in an open-minded way.

continued

Table AB.5 Continued

Anchor Standard	Code	Grade Level Outcome
Diversity 9	DI.9–12.9	I relate to and build connections with other people by showing them empathy, respect, and understanding, regardless of our similarities or differences.
Diversity 10	DI.9–12.10	I understand that diversity includes the impact of unequal power relations on the development of group identities and cultures.
Justice 11	JU.9–12.11	I relate to all people as individuals rather than representatives of groups and can identify stereotypes when I see or hear them.
Justice 12	JU.9–12.12	I can recognize, describe, and distinguish unfairness and injustice at different levels of society.
Justice 13	JU.9–12.13	I can explain the short- and long-term impact of biased words and behaviors and unjust practices, laws, and institutions that limit the rights and freedoms of people based on their identity groups.
Justice 14	JU.9–12.14	I am aware of the advantages and disadvantages I have in society because of my membership in different identity groups, and I know how this has affected my life.
Justice 15	JU.9–12.15	I can identify figures, groups, events, and a variety of strategies and philosophies relevant to the history of social justice around the world.
Action 16	AC.9–12.16	I express empathy when people are excluded or mistreated because of their identities and concern when I personally experience bias.
Action 17	AC.9–12.17	I take responsibility for standing up to exclusion, prejudice, and injustice.
Action 18	AC.9–12.18	I have the courage to speak up to people when their words, actions, or views are biased and hurtful, and I will communicate with respect even when we disagree.
Action 19	AC.9–12.19	I stand up to exclusion, prejudice, and discrimination, even when it's not popular or easy or when no one else does.
Action 20	AC.9–12.20	I will join with diverse people to plan and carry out collective action against exclusion, prejudice, and discrimination, and we will be thoughtful and creative in our actions in order to achieve our goals.

School Culture Triage Survey

Scoring: 1 = Never; 2 = Rarely; 3 = Sometimes; 4 = Often;
5 = Always or almost always.

Professional Collaboration

1. Teachers and staff discuss instructional strategies and curriculum issues.
2. Teachers and staff work together to develop the school schedule.
3. Teachers and staff are involved in the decision-making process with regard to materials and resources.
4. The student behavior code is a result of collaboration and consensus among staff.
5. The planning and organizational time allotted to teachers and staff is used to plan as collective units/teams rather than as separate individuals.

Affiliative Collegiality

1. Teachers and staff tell stories of celebrations that support the school's values.
2. Teachers and staff visit/talk/meet outside of the school to enjoy each other's company.
3. Our school reflects a true "sense" of community.
4. Our school schedule reflects frequent communication opportunities for teachers and staff.
5. Our school supports and appreciates the sharing of new ideas by members of our school.
6. There is a rich and robust tradition of rituals and celebrations including holidays, special events, and recognition of goal attainment.

Self-Determination/Efficacy

1. When something is not working in our school, the faculty and staff predict and prevent rather than react and repair.
2. School members are interdependent and value each other.
3. Members of our school community seek alternatives to problems/issues rather than repeating what we have always done.
4. Members of our school community seek to define the problem/issue rather than blame others.

5. The school staff is empowered to make instructional decisions rather than waiting for supervisors to tell them what to do.
6. People work here because they enjoy and choose to be here.

Scoring the School Culture Triage Survey

The lowest triage score is 17 and the highest score is 85. After using the triage questions in several program evaluations, our data suggests the following:

17–40   Critical and immediate attention necessary. Conduct a full-scale assessment of your school's culture and invest all available resources in repairing and healing the culture.

41–59   Modifications and improvements are necessary. Begin with a more intense assessment of your school's culture to determine which area is in most need of improvement.

60–75   Monitor and maintain making positive adjustments.

76–85   Amazing! We have never had a score higher than 75!

Before engaging in an elaborate and extensive analysis of the school culture, this quick assessment of current status can assist in determining the wise allocation of time and resources.

Reference

Wagner, C., & Masden-Copas, P. (2002). An audit of the culture starts with two handy tools. *Journal of Staff Development, 23*(3), 42–53.

Index

Page numbers in **bold** denote tables, those in *italics* denote figures.